R Courtois

Christ's Teaching And Our Religious Divisions

R Courtois

Christ's Teaching And Our Religious Divisions

ISBN/EAN: 9783743462779

Manufactured in Europe, USA, Canada, Australia, Japa

Cover: Foto ©Lupo / pixelio.de

Manufactured and distributed by brebook publishing software (www.brebook.com)

R Courtois

Christ's Teaching And Our Religious Divisions

CHRIST'S TEACHING

AND OUR

RELIGIOUS DIVISIONS

BY THE
REV. R. COURTOIS,
B.A. of the Université de France

"Rogo . . . ut omnes unum sint."—JOAN. xvii. 20 21.

London and Leamington
ART AND BOOK COMPANY
New York, Cincinnati, Chicago: BENZIGER BROTHERS
1898

INTRODUCTORY.

The "Times" of May 13th, 1884, asserted that in England alone there were some 700 *sects*. Each of these claims to follow the teaching of Christ, but some hold about it views diametrically opposed to those accepted by others. Our Lord taught only one doctrine, it is therefore evident that all those views cannot be the expression of it : if some are correct, the others in contradiction to them must be wrong; and as a consequence such Denominations as follow the latter cannot be said to know what Christ taught, in other words, they are *ignorant* of one or more points of His teaching.

Now man by the instinct of his very nature loves truth and dislikes error : is there a means of satisfying that desire and finding the *truth* about Christ's doctrine ? Ignorance is responsible for most of our religious divisions : is there any possibility of dispelling it, of getting all men to know what Our Divine Lord taught and of thus putting an end to those unhappy divisions?

We purpose to show in this little book that Christ Himself has made the thing possible. And this we intend to prove by appealing to a guide which all possess viz., common sense or *reason*, and by asking that guide what must have been the will of God our Saviour with regard to the doctrine He taught, and then what means He must have chosen to bring about the result intended. We shall also make an appeal to *history* and show from records of the past that both the intention of our Lord and the means chosen to carry it out, were, as a matter of fact, precisely what reason tells us they must have been. We trust to make it clear that Christ has appointed a means for all to find the truth about His teaching, and to be of one mind both as to what He wishes us to believe and as to the way He desires that we should worship and serve Him.

May Christ Jesus grant that we all make use of the means He has provided, so that we may at last all agree as to what He really did teach, believe every truth He taught, reject all human addition to His teaching, and thus see the end of our religious divisions.

DUMFRIES,
St. Andrew's Day, 1897.

CONTENTS.

CHAPTER	PAGE
SUMMARY	vii-viii

I.—CHRIST THE DIVINE TEACHER .   1-6

II.—CHRIST WISHES ALL MEN TO KNOW, ACCEPT AND LIVE UP TO HIS TEACHING .   7-18

III.—CHRIST MUST HAVE PROVIDED MANKIND WITH THE MEANS OF KNOWING HIS TEACHING. VARIOUS OPINIONS AS TO THE NATURE OF THAT MEANS . .   19-32

IV.—THE MEANS THAT REASON TELLS US CHRIST MUST HAVE APPOINTED, SINCE HE WISHES MEN TO ARRIVE AT A REAL KNOWLEDGE OF HIS TEACHING . .   33-48

V.—HISTORY TEACHES THAT CHRIST APPOINTED THE VERY MEANS OF ENABLING MEN TO KNOW HIS DOCTRINE, WHICH COMMON SENSE DECLARES HE MUST HAVE CHOSEN   49-99

VI.—WHERE THAT MEANS IS TO BE FOUND AT THE PRESENT DAY   100-105

CONCLUSION   105-110

SUMMARY.

Introduction.—Erroneous views about Christ's doctrine are the cause of most of our Religious divisions; we purpose to show from common sense and history that there is a means of all knowing what our Lord taught and so holding the same belief (p. iii.)

Chapter I.—The New Testament, a trustworthy historical document, tells us that our Lord taught a religious doctrine (p. 1); indeed nineteen centuries have looked upon Him as a founder and therefore a Teacher of Religion

EMENDANDA.

Page viii. *line* 40, *for* points *read* point.
,, 19, ,, 18, *for* them *read* us.
,, 21, ,, 15, *for* the individual. Others again who read it maintain *read* the individual who reads it. Others again maintain.
,, 21, ,, 20, *for* on His doctrine *read* as His doctrine.
,, 23, ,, 2, *for* let *read* left.
,, 25, ,, 23, *for* from this we can only conclude that we have enough text to, *read* from this text we can only conclude that we have enough to.
,, 30, ,, 28, *for* regret *read* reject.
,, 30, ,, 31, *for* Migne called, *read* Migne, and called.
,, 63, ,, 15, *for* no man lay, *read* no man can lay.

brought within reach of all, except through men acting as teachers (p. 33). Nor can the end in view be attained if our Lord has not granted a special body of teachers exclusive authority to impart His doctrine and does not enable them to offer men a conclusive proof that they have such divine authority (p. 34); if, besides, He does not preserve them as a body from erring in doctrine (p. 40), and has not placed over both masters and disciples some supreme authority (p. 41), which He must,

SUMMARY.

Introduction.—Erroneous views about Christ's doctrine are the cause of most of our Religious divisions; we purpose to show from common sense and history that there is a means of all knowing what our Lord taught and so holding the same belief (p. iii.)

Chapter I.—The New Testament, a trustworthy historical document, tells us that our Lord taught a religious doctrine (p. 1); indeed nineteen centuries have looked upon Him as a founder and therefore a Teacher of Religion (p. 4).

Chapter II.—Now it would be strange if, having Himself taught a religious doctrine, He did not wish all men to know it (p. 7). Accordingly, it is and has been the conviction in every age that He binds all men to embrace His Religion (p. 7); and the New Testament explicitly tells us that He wishes (p. 8) nay, obliges them to know, accept and live up to His teaching (p. 11).

Chapter III.—But if so, He must have provided mankind with the means of knowing it, for "He who wills the end wills the means" (p. 19); in reality all agree that He has given men such means, although they disagree as to its nature (p. 20). But reason tells us that the means appointed must be such as to enable all men to know His teaching, be sure of its tenets and all of one mind about them (p. 21). Consequently that means cannot be the New Testament alone (p. 22). or with an interior light and motion of the Holy Ghost (p. 29), or even with the writings of the Fathers (p. 30).

Chapter IV.—Reason finds that Christ's doctrine cannot be brought within reach of all, except through men acting as teachers (p. 33). Nor can the end in view be attained if our Lord has not granted a special body of teachers exclusive authority to impart His doctrine and does not enable them to offer men a conclusive proof that they have such divine authority (p. 34); if, besides, He does not preserve them as a body from erring in doctrine (p. 40), and has not placed over both masters and disciples some supreme authority (p. 41), which He must, in certain cases, preserve from falling into error (p. 42), and which reason finds should be vested in one man (p. 43). Under this arrangement no one should be considered as authorised by Christ as teacher, unless he is at least tacitly recognised as such by the head of the teaching body (p. 47).

Chapter V.—Now history tells us that Christ has done precisely what common sense finds He must have done. It tells us that our Lord has appointed an infallible teaching authority which He intends to exist till the end of time; for He has given a body of men, in the person of His Apostles, authority to teach His doctrine and even rule and govern the faithful (p. 49); He has granted them as a body a privilege of immunity from error in teaching matters of faith and morals (p. 52); and He means them to exist till the end of time as teachers and rulers (p 55); and to be till the end of ages infallible as a body (p. 58) History adds that He has placed the teachers and the learners under one infallible head, having chosen and appointed Peter as first pastor of the fold (p. 60), made him infallible in doctrine as supreme shepherd (p. 68), and meaning him to have successors endowed with the same prerogatives of supremacy (p. 71) and infallibility, till the end of the world (p. 79). From which it follows that the common and conclusive proof that a particular man is authorised by Christ as teacher, is the fact that he is at least tacitly recognised as such by Peter or his successors (p. 96).

Chapter VI.—Therefore there exists at the present day a means of knowing Christ's teaching and avoiding religious divisions. Now of all the teaching bodies of the present time, only one, the Catholic Church claims to be under an infallible head. The others deny even the existence of an infallible head in the Church of Christ (p. 100).

Conclusion—Therefore none of the others are authorised by Christ to teach His doctrine, and so they remain liable to error, and consequently should be ignored by any one wishing to know Christ's religion. Nay more, we should all accept the teachers and submit to the authority that both our common sense and history points out to us, in order not to be condemned by reason and by Him who said, " He that despiseth you, despiseth Me" (p. 105).

CHRIST'S TEACHING

AND

OUR RELIGIOUS DIVISIONS.

CHAPTER I.

CHRIST THE DIVINE TEACHER,

Pronounced as such by the New Testament.

No person who has studied the New Testament, and accepts the evidence of history, need be reminded of the fact that Jesus came as a Teacher of men. More than fifty times the evangelists tell us in so many words that Jesus was teaching; more than two hundred times they speak of His disciples; and in almost every page they show us our Lord acting in the capacity of Teacher of men, revealing to them truths which they could not otherwise have known, telling them what their duties were towards God and their neighbour, and what was to be the reward of their obedience and the punishment of their revolt and wickedness. His teaching as recorded in Holy Writ treats of such points as the existence and unity of *God*, His infinite perfection, His providence, His mercy towards man, the Trinity of the Divine Persons, the Divinity of the Son and of the Holy Ghost, the existence of angels and of devils, the Incarnation, the Passion and Redemption, the way to salvation, the existence and the operation of Grace, the union of souls with Christ, the spirituality and immortality of the *soul*, the resurrection of the body, judgment, the joys of *Heaven*, the pains and torments of *Hell*, etc. Christ moreover tells men what *obligations* they have to discharge towards God, their parents, superiors, inferiors, the poor, their enemies and sinners; He warns them to avoid unbelief, pride, ambition, vanity, hypocrisy, avarice, anger, cowardice, inconstancy, gluttony, impurity, human respect, scandal, even desires that tend towards an unlawful object; He urges them to aim at perfection, to practise faith, hope, charity towards God, religion, prayer, confidence in Divine Providence, generosity, charity towards men, meekness, purity of heart and intention, self-denial, chastity, humility, obedience, mortification, patience, prudence, etc. (Cf. Gospel, passim.) No one, He says, can enter into Heaven, unless he is born again of water and of the Holy Ghost (John iii. 5); any one who refuses to hear the Church must be treated as a heathen and publican (Matt. xviii. 17); if any one wish to enter into life, he must keep the commandments (Matt. xix. 17); if any one love Christ, he must keep His commandments (John xiv. 15); any man who has not on a wedding garment will be cast into exterior darkness, where there is weeping and gnashing of teeth (Matt. xxii. 11-13). Elsewhere He points out to men the *means* they must make use of in order to attain that sanctification which it is the will of God that all should possess (1 Thess iv. 3; 1 Tim. ii. 4); or to keep His commandments and thereby prove to Him both their submission and love (John xiv. 15). Amongst such means mentioned by our Lord, or by those who knew His teaching best, we find faith in Christ;[1] love;[2] vigilance and prayer;[3] baptism;[4] penance;[5] the remission of sin by the Apostles;[6] the Body and Blood of Christ;[7] the unction with oil made by the priests and accompanied with prayer;[8] the imposition of hands;[9] good works;[10] the grace of God, etc.[11]

Our Lord taking upon Himself the office of Teacher, must necessarily have been the most zealous, devoted and winning of masters, and His arguments must have proved the most convincing. We are therefore prepared to expect that, after a time, several of those who were privileged to listen to the words of wisdom that fell from His lips, should cleave to Him and become His *disciples*. St. John tells us that on one occasion about five thousand were following Him to a mountain (John vi. 10), which may give us an idea of the multitudes that crowded after Him through towns and country districts; the whole world was gone after Him, according to the

[1] John iii. 16. [2] John xiv. 23. [3] Matt. xxvi. 41.
[4] Mark xv. 16. [5] Luke xiii. 3. [6] John xx. 23.
[7] John vi. 54. [8] James 5. 15. [9] 2 Tim. vi. 6.
[10] James ii. 26. [11] Rom. vii. 23-25; Ephes. iv. 7.

Pharisees (John xii. 19). The influence He exercised was so great that it excited the admiration and respect of all, even of those who had come to apprehend Him. St. John relates that ministers sent by the Chief Priests and Pharisees to arrest Him came back alone, and could not refrain from expressing their admiration of Him to His very enemies. " Never did man speak like this man," they said to the Pharisees and Chief Priests (John vii. 46). Those who listened to Him wondered how He had acquired His knowledge (Mark vi. 2).

Amongst His followers and admirers there were some who were nearly always with Him, whom He would call His sheep and of whom He would name Himself the Shepherd (Matt. xii. 32 ; John x. 27-28). They formed truly one *society* with Him : He was the vine and they were the branches (John xv. 5). They were few at first, but soon multiplied; and indeed He intended that they should increase more and more ; for He compares them to a mustard seed (Matt. xiii. 31), and foretells that, as that grain, though the least of all seeds, becomes in time a tree, in like manner that society, composed of His Apostles and disciples, though small in its beginning, will increase and extend ; His wish was that all should become members of it, so that there should be but one fold and one shepherd. This flock is what He calls His Church, His " qahal," i.e. His chosen people, just as the Hebrews of old were God's " qahal," God's chosen people.[1] And this society of disciples had so far developed that, after His resurrection, He could appear to more than five hundred at once (2 Cor. xv. 16). If we can rely on the New Testament, we have every proof that Jesus not only made Himself the Teacher of men, but was listened to, admired, followed, and loved by them as a teacher.

Need we add that the New Testament is a book that can be relied upon as a *trustworthy hitsorical document* ? As such, its value, we must admit, has been questioned and even denied ; but the difficulties brought forward to disprove it, have been, time after time, discussed and satisfactorily dealt with. (See Vigouroux, Les Livres Saints et la Critique Rationaliste au XIX. Siècle. Paris : Roger et Chernoviz.) One reason why we may safely rely upon the information it contains is, that the New Testament, from the very

---

[1] See Levit. iv. 3 ; Num. xvi. 3, xx. 4 ; Exod. xix. 3, etc.

first appearance of its various parts, has been as much in the hands of orthodox Christians as of their adversaries, and has consequently had every safeguard against any substantial alteration. It has come down to us as the work of the first disciples of Christ, men who must have told the truth, for no earthly motive could have led them to concoct a false account of their Master's life; their veracity is indeed beyond a doubt, for the greater part of what they relate took place before many witnesses, whose hostility would have at once seized upon any opportunity of exposing their want of truth.

Nineteen Centuries have considered Christ as a Founder of Religion. What this implies.

We need not appeal to the New Testament to show that our Lord made Himself the Teacher of men eighteen centuries ago. The word "Christian" is a sufficient proof of the fact. Those who bear that name profess to be the disciples of Christ, and implicitly acknowledge and proclaim that He founded a religion. This, moreover, is not the testimony of a few ignorant people, living centuries after the death of our Saviour: it is the evidence of millions of men, who, for the last eighteen hundred years have all proclaimed the same fact from the midst of tortures, as well as from the chairs of the most famous Universities; it is the testimony of Catholics, as well as of Non-Catholics; of Christians of the nineteenth, as well as of the second century; it is even that of Pagans and of enemies of the Christian name, given soon after the death of Christ (Josephus, Antiq. lib. 18; Celsus apud Origen. lib. 1); every one knows that these early adversaries never questioned the fact that our Lord was the Founder of the religion called after His Name; they admitted it, for they sneered at Christians because they were the disciples of a crucified Galilean. Modern rationalists cannot account for an evidence of this kind, unless they acknowledge that *Christ did really establish a religion*.

If all do and must confess this truth, even without consulting the New Testament, then they implicitly admit that the Redeemer actually gave to His disciples a *body of doctrine*, and imposed on them *obligations*, calculated to enable them to know and worship God. One could hardly conceive a religion without religious doctrines and certain religious duties. And if Christ imposed obligations upon man, one must conclude that He also secured for him the *means to fulfil them* : for, being God and infinitely just, He could not ask him to do anything beyond his power.

We need hardly add that He constituted Himself the *teacher* of that Religion, as no one can be called a founder unless he has taught the doctrine and obligations that are its essential parts.

That Teacher is God Himself : therefore from the mere fact that, in His mercy, He undertook to preach to men a religion, we may feel sure that He enabled them to *know and worship God*, as no other Master could have done. Being infinitely good, and knowing how important it was that the human mind should be satisfied at least on points of great *practical consequence*, He must undoubtedly have thrown a powerful light on such important points as the following, which are, so to speak, the basis of religion. Why are we in this world, and what are we expected to do while in it ? Are we here only to grow rich and seek comfort ? Have we any duties towards God, our Maker ? Does He care for our homage ? Does He take an interest in us ? Does it matter how we worship Him, or are there forms of worship that He approves of, others that He condemns ? What is the best way to honour and please Him ? If we honour Him, will he ever reward us ? What will the reward be ? How long will it last ? If we live as if there were no God, shall we be punished ? What will the chastisement be, and what its duration ? We feel a craving for life and happiness : will that craving never be satisfied, whatever we may do ? We feel bound to obey the dictates of our conscience : is this a mere matter of imagination, or is there a real obligation to listen to its voice ? What will be the result if we follow or if we reject its guidance ? Of these and other similar questions, it is most important for men of all times to have a solution ; and, no doubt, Christ gave it to His disciples eighteen hundred years ago, since He undertook to teach them a religion, *i.e.*, enabled them to know and worship God.

Conclusion.

Both from the New Testament and from the accepted fact that our Lord founded a religion, we know that He appeared amongst men as a Divine Teacher ; and, from the little we read of Him in the New Testament, as well as from what our reason can surmise, it is evident that His teaching must have given an answer to all the most important and practical questions. We may therefore lawfully conclude that nothing can be more *desirable* and *profitable* than *to know what He taught*, and follow the directions He gave, eighteen centuries ago. Should we also infer that He must have intended His teaching, and the religion He founded, not only for the Jews, but for all men, and that, as a consequence, He has certainly provided them with the means of knowing what truths He taught, what obligations He imposed on mankind, and what means of sanctification He appointed ? These are points that we must now consider.

CHAPTER II.

CHRIST WISHES ALL MEN TO KNOW, ACCEPT, AND LIVE UP TO, HIS TEACHING.

How useful, important and perfect our Divine Lord's teaching must have been, we can easily understand from the fact that He is God, and from what we read of it in the New Testament, of which we gave a summary at the beginning of our first chapter. It is consequently but natural that we should ask the question whether Christ intended His teaching only for the Jews with whom He lived, or for all mankind as well. To our mind, there can be but one answer to such a question : Christ wished and still wishes all men of all times and countries to know, accept, and live up to, His teaching.

I.—It would be strange if He did not wish it.

Jesus Christ might have spoken through another Moses or through Prophets, if His desire was to establish a religion for one nation only. The fact that He taught it Himself, leads one to think that the new religion must be meant for all. His bounty being infinite, since He did not disdain to become a Teacher, to throw light upon so many important problems, and to enable men by His own lessons to know and worship God, reason concludes that He undoubtedly wishes all to benefit by His teaching and directions, and therefore to embrace His religion.

However, Christ is free to dispose of His gifts as He chooses, so that, whatever reason may anticipate and conjecture, we can hardly feel certain of our conclusion, unless He has Himself expressly told us what His intention was. This our Saviour has done.

II.—It is the conviction of all that He wishes it.

It has been the general conviction, ever since the first days of Christianity, that our Lord desires all men to embrace

His religion; nay, that all are bound to be Christians, that is, disciples of Christ.[1] Now nothing but the fact that either Christ, or His Apostles in His Name, gave rise to such a conviction by their teaching, can account for its existence through the course of ages.

III.—The New Testament explicitly says that He wishes all men to know and accept His teaching.

That most trustworthy of historical documents, the New Testament, tells us most emphatically that Jesus Christ not only wishes men to accept His teaching, and become His disciples, but commands them to do so.

1. That He desires not only the Jews, but all men of all times and countries to embrace His religion, is evident from *the mission He gives* to His Apostles: " Go ye into the whole world and preach the Gospel to every creature " (Mark xvi. 15-16); "Teach ye all nations . . . to observe all things whatsoever I have commanded you " (Matt. xxviii. 19-20). If you will realise how earnest His desire is, consider for a moment that, while thus sending His Apostles, Jesus knew what they would have to suffer in fulfilling their mission: " They shall deliver you up to be afflicted, and shall put you to death ; and you shall be hated by all nations for My Name's sake" (Matt. xxiv. 9-10); "They will scourge you in their synagogues" (Matt. x. 17; Luke xxi. 12; John xvi. 20); " The hour cometh that whosoever killeth you, will think that he does a service to God " (John xvi. 2). Yet, all the time, these men whom He was sending to preach the Gospel and die for Him, were His friends (John xvi. 15). Is not this a clear proof of the earnestness of His desire that His doctrine should be taught and listened to throughout the whole world, for although preaching meant persecution and death, He sends His very friends upon this mission ? And to whom are they sent ? To *all nations,* to *every creature* that will ever live, until the end of time : " Teach all nations . . . I am with you all days even to the consummation of the world " (Matt. xxviii. 19-20). Speaking of the sheep that are not of His

[1] See Tertullian, De Bapt. c. 8'; Hieron. Epist. 15 ad Damasum et Dialog. adv. Lucifer. n. 22 ; Cyprian, iii. De Unitate Ecclesiæ ; Gaudentium Brixianum, Tract. I. De Lectione Evangelica ; et anonymum sæculi iii. adv. Novatianum ; Gallandi Bibl. tom. iii. p. 371.

fold, He had already said : " Them also must I bring, and they will hear My voice," wishing of course to convey that they would know His doctrine and live up to it (John x. 16) ; and we now see Him sending His Apostles to those sheep, that they may enter His fold.

A striking proof of that desire is given in the Book of the Acts (x. 3, 6, 20), when God sends an angel and an Apostle to *Cornelius the Centurion*, in order to teach him the doctrine of Christ. Cornelius was a man leading a good, moral and upright life ; but God wished him to know the doctrine of His Divine Son and conform his life thereto.

And what are His Apostles to teach ? His religion purely and simply ; not only faith in Him, but also the observance of His precepts ; not merely the fundamental points of His doctrine, but His Gospel in the broadest sense. " Preach the *Gospel;* . . . teach ye all nations . . . to observe *all things* whatsoever I have commanded you."

What this wish implies.

But Christ taught only one Gospel, one doctrine or religious system. Therefore, if He wishes all men to know that one Gospel, we may infer that He is desirous they should all believe *the same truths*, and be under the same obligations ; we may also conclude that He wishes them to have a real knowledge of them, that is to say, to *know for certain* what He taught, what obligations He imposed, and what means, if any, He appointed to enable men to fulfil those obligations and to sanctify themselves.

Yes ; and the New Testament tells us that His wish is exactly what we infer. " Other sheep I have," says our Lord, " that are not of this fold. Them also must I bring ; . . . and there shall be one fold, one shepherd " (John x. 16) ; " And not for them only do I pray, but for them also who, through their word, shall believe in me, *that they all may be one* " (John xvii. 20-21). But union and unity cannot exist amongst His disciples, if certain doctrines are believed in by some as true and sure, but rejected by others as false or doubtful, or if certain obligations are considered by some as binding, and rejected by others as doubtful or as non-existing : therefore, in wishing His disciples to be one, He evidently wishes them all to believe the same truths, to consider the same obligations as binding, and to feel no uncertainty on that head.

2. But, it may be asked, do we not put a wrong and prejudiced construction on our Lord's words, when we take them to mean that He desired all men of every age to know what He taught, to believe the same truths, to be of one mind and quite certain about His teaching, as well as about the relative importance of each and all the obligations He imposed? Our answer is emphatically "No," and for the reason that the *Apostles* put the very same construction on our Lord's words as we do ourselves.

They *understood* that Christ wished His doctrine to be known and accepted by *all men*; for St. Paul says: "God our Saviour will have all men to be saved and to come to the knowledge of truth" (1 Tim. ii. 4). They all went and preached the Gospel, not only in Jerusalem and Judea, but through the whole world. On the day of Pentecost, Peter addresses the Jews and makes three thousand converts; and a little later, he makes five thousand more (Acts ii. 41; iv. 4). A few years after the death of Christ, St. Paul writes to the Colossians (i. 6) that the Gospel has come unto them, as it has to the whole world, and is growing and bringing forth fruit; and to the Romans (i. 8) he announces the joyful fact that their faith is spoken of everywhere. St. Paul himself preached our Lord's doctrine in Palestine, Syria, Asia Minor, Thrace, Macedonia and Greece, and reached Rome after founding Churches in every one of those provinces (Acts passim). We learn from the first epistle of St. Peter that there were disciples of Jesus in Pontus, Galatia, Cappadocia, Asia and Bithynia (1 Pet. i. 1). The zeal of the Apostles in carrying out His known desires lasted as long as their lives; it came to an end only when, in death, they rested from their labours. In order to fulfil the precept they had received, to teach all nations and to preach the Gospel to every creature, they regularly appointed bishops to continue their work (Matthias, Paul, Barnabas, Timothy, Mark, etc.; Acts xiv. 22; Philipp. i. 1), and told them also to preach and appoint other bishops (Acts xx. 28; 1 Tim. iv. 14; v. 22; 2 Tim. iv. 2; Tit. i. 5; ii. 15).

They understood that men were not to guess, but really to *know* Christ's doctrine; for St. Paul says that our Saviour took care that men should not be " tossed to and fro, and carried about with every wind of doctrine" (Ephes. iv. 11-16). They understood that men were to be taught nothing but what Jesus Himself had taught, that is to say, *the one doctrine of Christ*: "There is but one Lord, one Faith, one Baptism," says St. Paul (Ephes. iv. 5-6); "If any one preach you a Gospel besides that which you have received, let him be anathema" (Galat. i. 8-9); nay, "though we or an angel from heaven preach a gospel to you, besides that which you have received, let him be anathema" (Galat. i. 8). St. Paul knew that what he had taught was Christ's doctrine, and that any one setting forth a different belief would not be preaching as Christ had done; he even goes so far as to pronounce a curse upon any one who would take from, or add one jot to, that same doctrine. Some being of opinion that the Jewish ceremonial was still binding upon Christians, the Apostles held a council in Jerusalem, and condemned that view: an example of the discipline of the early Church, which serves to show us how careful were those who had received their mission immediately from Christ Himself, lest any corruption of His teaching should be introduced (Acts xv. 1, 5-30).

We need not add that the successors of the Apostles preached the Gospel, as the Apostles did, and moreover, like their predecessors also, condemned any one trying to introduce new ideas, or denying the truths taught by our Lord. "We are but of yesterday," writes Tertullian, "and we fill your cities, islands, castles, camps, tribes, the palace, the senate and the forum, and we leave you only your temples" (Apologet. c. 37). We shall see later on how attempts to alter the teaching of Christ were checked in the Church. What we have said is enough for our present purpose; we think we have shown sufficiently clearly that those who had every means of knowing the mind of Christ understood, as we do, that He wished all men to know, and to be all of one mind, and quite certain about His teaching.

IV.—The New Testament tells us that He not only wishes but even binds men to know and accept His teaching.

We said above that Christ's desire that all men should know and accept His doctrine was so earnest that He actually placed them under the obligation of knowing and accepting it ; and this we proceed to prove.

We may sum up His instructions by saying (1) that He informed men of the existence of a number of obligations, at the same time pointing out to them the means whereby they could be fulfilled, and (2) that He taught them also a certain number of truths to be believed.

1. Now as to the *obligations* which He imposed and made known to men, as well as to the means of fulfilling them, it is evident that if the word has any meaning at all, all the "obligations" imposed on men by Christ are binding ; it is evident also that, if He offers us *means* or helps that are indispensable to fulfil those obligations or to save our souls (for this is clearly one of our strictest duties), we are bound by common sense as well as by our Lord's commands to make use of them.

But here follows a practical consequence : while some of those obligations may bind only in a small degree, others may do so under pain of severe punishment, such as damnation, in the case of any man wilfully neglecting to fulfil them ; likewise, while some of the means Christ offers us, enabling us to fulfil those duties and thereby save our souls, may be only useful, others may be absolutely indispensable, so that anyone wilfully neglecting to employ them, may be supposed to have the will not to fulfil his obligations and to lose his soul. Such being the case, we are evidently bound by Christ and by reason itself to make due *enquiries* in order to find out whether He intend certain obligations to be thus strictly binding, and whether certain means He wishes us to make use of be indispensable for the fulfilment of such strictly binding duties and for the salvation of our souls. To remain wilfully ignorant on those two points would indeed be tantamount to despising God's authority, or being willing to lose our souls, which conduct reason and God cannot but condemn.

Therefore, this is how we stand with regard both to our obligations (including that of saving our souls), and to the means of fulfilling them : Christ binds us, on the one hand, to fulfil all the obligations He has imposed on mankind, and to employ whatever means are necessary to fulfil them ; on the other hand, if we do not precisely know what those obligations and means may be, but at the same time, believe that

He has, or may have, imposed obligations on men, we are bound by our Lord and common sense to make reasonable inquiries in order to escape that condemnation which, in a matter of such great importance, must be meted out to wilful ignorance.

2. This leads us to ask the question whether our Lord made it one of our obligations to *know and accept everything He taught*, and if so, how far this obligation binds us. We think that the following may be a correct answer.

A. Christ forbids us *to deny* any even of the minor points of His doctrine, when He says : " He that believeth not shall be condemned " (Mark xvi. 16). And no wonder, as this is only what justice would require. To deny what we rightly or wrongly look upon as part of Christ's doctrine, unimportant though that point may appear, is to be guilty of a most grievous offence : for the denying anything we consider He has taught, is tantamount to saying that the point we deny is not true, and consequently that Christ did not know or did not tell the truth, which is blasphemy.

We are not guilty of the same offence, if we are ignorant that the point we deny is part of Christ's teaching; yet our denial is radically wrong, though we consider the point we deny as contrary to truth. Our case is after all that of a man who denies a truth, or tells a falsehood, through ignorance : such a one may be blameless, and even praiseworthy in the eyes of God, for refusing to believe what he considers to be untrue; yet God, while approving of the man following his conscience, does not, at the same time, approve of the falsehood, or of the truth being denied. In His eyes, to tell a falsehood or to deny a truth is radically wrong, and consequently never to be approved of.

Of course, we should actually be guilty in the eyes of God, if we deny what we believe to be true, although we may not regard what we deny as being revealed by Christ; for our reason (or rather God, who speaks to us through our reason,) forbids such denial, and commands us to accept as true what we deem to be so.

We must therefore conclude that, since it is in itself wrong and forbidden by God to deny any point, even of minor importance, that happens to have been part of the teaching of Christ, nothing can ever justify our denial of the smallest article of His doctrine: ignorance alone saves such a denial from being a most grievous offence. Consequently, when we hear it proposed that the numerous Christian denominations should each and all make certain concessions to bring about that union for which our Divine Lord prayed after the last supper (John xvii. 20, 29), we must condemn such a scheme, if it implies the denial of the least point taught by Jesus Christ, or of the least particle of truth. Desirable though that union may be, God cannot approve of its being bought at the expense of truth, of our Lord's doctrine, or even of what we rightly or wrongly believe to be Christ's doctrine: never will the end justify the means.

B. The same reasons which tend to establish that Christ forbids us to deny any article of His teaching, prove also that He binds us to believe any truth He may choose, or may have chosen, to make known to us. Therefore we are bound to have what is called *implicit faith*, that is to say, to be ever ready and willing to believe Him, and whatever truths He may propose to our belief. That we are bound to be always in that disposition of mind is obvious; for to be otherwise would mean that we already call in question, if not deny, His infinite knowledge or truthfulness, which, as we have just said, would be nothing less than blasphemy; it might also imply that we think He is not anxious to be believed, and consequently is not a real lover of truth—another form of blasphemy.

C. But should we go no further? Should we not say that, of the truths taught or revealed by our Divine Saviour, He binds us *to know and believe explicitly* at least a certain number? No doubt, to know and understand everything He did would hardly be possible. St. John writes that " There are . . . many . . . things which Jesus did, which, if they were written every one, the world itself . . . would not be able to contain the books that should be written " (John xxi. 25). But we have our Lord's words, by which He obliges all men to know at least a certain number of the truths He taught, and to believe them : " He that heareth you heareth Me ; . . . he that believeth and is baptised shall be saved, but he that believeth not shall be condemned " (Matt. xvi. 15, 16). In these words Christ gives men the strongest possible motives to accept, from the lips of His Apostles, His heavenly doctrine; He manifests His anxiety that they should do so, by threatening to condemn them, if they do not: He actually declares that they are absolutely bound to believe, since He makes their salvation or damnation depend on their acceptance or non-acceptance of His teaching. And such a sanction clearly implies a most strict obligation. But the context plainly shows that men are not merely bound to believe the Apostles after a vague and empty fashion, but are also obliged to accept what they say; for it is evident that those who "hear" the Apostles, hear them teaching; and those who are told to "believe," are naturally ordered to believe "what they are taught," which supposes in them a certain knowledge and understanding of what the Apostles say. Now, if the words of our Lord, "He that believeth not shall be condemned," imply that men must believe something, we may rest assured that we must believe the *chief truths* He taught, for his words should refer to such, if they apply to any truths at all. If we do not know what these are, or what we have to believe in particular, we are strictly bound to make every reasonable *enquiry*, that we may thus find out what we must know and accept, and thereby avoid being condemned for wilful neglect and ignorance. St. Paul mentions two of these truths when he says: "Without faith it is impossible to please God; for he that cometh to God must believe that He is, and is a rewarder to them that seek Him" (Hebrews xi. 6): we have here clearly expressed the obligation of "explicit belief" in the existence of God and in a remuneration. Elsewhere we see the necessity of believing (and therefore of knowing) the mysteries of the Blessed Trinity and of the Incarnation (John xvii. 3; xiv. 6; Acts iv. 12), though that necessity is not so clearly brought out. But there may be other articles of belief equally necessary, and this possibility renders it needful for us to make enquiry.

Obligations may arise also from the nature of the truths taught by Christ, so that to remain wilfully ignorant of His teaching may be equivalent to remaining wilfully ignorant of our duties, which would make us responsible for neglecting them and possibly result in our damnation. To give two illustrations of this obligation to enquire: let us suppose a man does not believe in Baptism, because he is ignorant of what Christ said about it; all he knows is that some people mention it as one of the conditions of salvation, while others deny its necessity. Will not God and reason condemn that man, if he does not think it worth his while to make enquiries as to what our Lord taught on that point? If Baptism be indispensable for salvation, it is clearly incumbent upon him to receive it, since reason as well as God commands him to save his soul; if he wilfully omits to receive it, because he wilfully neglects to make enquiries, he is evidently acting against common sense, and can only expect to be condemned by God for his wilful negligence and ignorance. Take another man who is ignorant of what Christ meant, when He said: "This is My Body . . . This is My Blood . . . Do this for a commemoration of Me" (Luke xxii. 19, 20); he knows what the two hundred and seventy-five million Catholics and all the Eastern Communities together with the Greek and Russian Churches understand by those words,—namely that priests can change bread and wine into the Body and Blood of Christ,—while nearly all the other Christian denominations deny that power.[1] Will such a man be justified in remaining absolutely indifferent, and in making no enquiries to find out what Christ meant, and whether He did or did not give such a power to man? Reason says that to remain indifferent, not to make enquiries, or endeavour to solve one's doubts, is most offensive and injurious to God. If priests truly have that wonderful power, then under the appearances of bread and wine, at a given moment, there is really present he Body and Blood of our Lord, the Divine Person of Christ, the Saviour who shed His Blood on Calvary for every one of us, the Judge of the living and the dead; and, of course, we should render Him our homage, adore, thank, and honour Him the more as He almost annihilates Himself in order to be with us: whereas, if priests do not possess that faculty, He is not present; but their belief has for centuries led many millions of

---

[1] "We have it on the authority of the Osservatore Romano, that it results from the estimates made by the various missionaries, that the total number of the members of the Catholic Church is actually between two hundred and seventy-five and three hundred millions" (Tablet, Oct. 17, 1885). All the Protestant Denominations are supposed to number 140 millions, according to Mulhall's Dictionary of Statistics, ed. 1892.

Catholics and of eastern Non-Catholics, etc., to treat as God what is only bread and wine; they have acted, it may be, with every good intention: nevertheless, if they are mistaken their mistake has led and still leads them to a most deplorable act, for which all Christian denominations ought to offer a reparation to God. In fact, the good of the community would almost demand the cessation of this abuse, seeing how much ill-feeling is aroused by anti-Catholic lecturers, who justify their violent language on the ground that Catholics are idolaters. If Christ be there, then to remain indifferent, not to make enquiries, is wilfully to refuse a homage due to Him; if He be not there, to remain indifferent, and make no enquiries, is also wilfully to deny Him a homage due to Him, which practically renders that man equally guilty in the eyes of God.

"He that believeth not shall be condemned" (Matt. xvi. 15, 16). From this condemnation, *they alone* can be exempt who have never been taught, or are incapable of instruction, or have never in any way thought of the obligation, which exists, to believe and, consequently, to know Christ's teaching, or who, after reasonable enquiries, have failed to discover what they had to believe and do. With this exception and the one mentioned above (p. 13) no one can be saved, unless he fulfil all the grave obligations imposed upon him, and revealed by Christ or reason, and unless he use such means of sanctification as Christ or reason may declare to be indispensable, believe implicitly the whole doctrine of Christ, and explicitly know and accept at least such points of it as are of greater importance; in other words, unless he know, accept, and live up to, the teaching of Christ.

Consequences.

But if our Lord actually *binds* men to know, accept, and live up to His teaching, it is clear that, as we have said previously, He at least *wishes* them to know, accept, and live up to it. Consequently, we may draw the following conclusions:

1. It is Christ's wish that all should know for certain, and be of one mind about, His teaching.
2. Since He wills His entire doctrine to be known, He must necessarily wish man to acquire as complete a knowledge as lies in his power.

3. It must be desirable and profitable for all to know as much of Christ's doctrine as possible; for, since He, who does nothing uselessly, thought proper to teach, and wishes all men to know and to live up to His instructions, it cannot but be desirable and profitable for them to comply with His desires.

4. Christians, above all, should aim at knowing at least the chief points of our Saviour's teaching. What we have just said of the whole doctrine, is evidently more true of its chief points; and what is applicable to all men, is still more so to a Christian, that is to a disciple of Christ: the reason is that no one can rightly claim the title of Christian, if he do not know and put into practice His doctrine, or, take the trouble to find it out, as far as he can, so as to act up to his belief.

5. As Christ not only wishes, but actually binds men to know, accept and live up to His teaching, not to comply with His commands may in certain cases endanger salvation.

CHAPTER III.

CHRIST MUST HAVE PROVIDED MANKIND WITH THE MEANS OF KNOWING HIS TEACHING. VARIOUS OPINIONS AS TO THE NATURE OF THAT MEANS.

Article I.—Christ must have provided mankind with the means of knowing His teaching.

IF, as was shown in the last chapter, and as most of our readers have no doubt always believed, Christ wishes all men to know, not to say, accept and live up to His teaching, it follows that He must have given them the means of knowing it. As He taught but one religious system, and made no contradictory statements on any given point, it follows also that the means of knowing what He taught must, so far as it is concerned, enable us to have a real knowledge of, and be all of one mind about, the various points of His teaching, or, as St. Paul says, prevent us from being "tossed to and fro, and carried about with every wind of doctrine" (Ephes. iv. 11-16), and lead them to have all one and the same faith (Ephes. iv. 5, 6 ; see John xvii. 20, 21). We do not say that all men making use of this means will actually know His teaching, feel no uncertainty about it, and have all the same faith ; but we hold that the means provided by Him must be able to produce that result, though, as a matter of fact, man's wickedness or want of ordinary intelligence may now and then render it practically powerless and inefficacious. For, unless Christ enables us to have all the same faith, and feel no uncertainty about His doctrine, it cannot be said that He provides us with the means of truly knowing what He taught.

Now, the reason why we conclude—from the fact that He wishes all men to know His teaching—that He must have given them the means to know it, is based upon this axiom that *He who wills the end wills the means.* Of course, if Christ were not God, or if we had those means otherwise, this conclusion might not be justified : I might, for example, wish a friend to see Paris, without being able, or without its being considered in any way obligatory on my part, to furnish him with the means of seeing it. But with Christ the case is different ; if men cannot of themselves attain the end He wishes, He must enable them to do so, since He is all-powerful; otherwise He would be inconsistent. On the other hand, it is evident that the truths, the obligations, and the means of fulfilling them cannot be guessed or surmised by men, since Christ came, among other reasons, for the purpose of instructing them on these various points. This, we think, justifies our assertion that He must have provided mankind with the means of knowing what He taught, for He Himself instructed none but the Jews, and His voice ceased to be heard in this world eighteen centuries ago. And since, in wishing men to know His doctrine, He implicitly, and indeed explicitly, desires that they should feel certain and be all of one mind about its tenets, He must have provided them with the means of obtaining the two-fold result, firmness of belief and unity of faith.

Moreover, even if men " thought " that they had some other suitable way of acquiring that knowledge, the mere fact of His having appointed a different one would be enough to show that their opinion is wrong, as God does nothing uselessly ; at all events, they should be disposed to give preference to the means provided by Christ, as acting otherwise would be, to say the least, unwise, imprudent and certainly against His wishes, if not commands. On this there can hardly be any diversity of opinion.

Article II.—Various Opinions as to the Nature of that Means.

But the case is different when we come to determine what are the means appointed by Christ to obtain the end He had in view.

However, long as the research may be, we should all feel anxious to know what Christ taught (p. 18), and we must all fulfil our obligations (p. 12 and seq.) of knowing and believing explicitly certain truths (p. 14 and seq.), and consequently make reasonable enquiries, if we do not know what they are (p. 12, 15 and 17) ; therefore it is a matter of necessity to weigh the various opinions, as there seems to be no other course left open, whereby to ascertain which of them, if any, offers us the right solution. As a matter of fact we have every chance of not working in vain and of finding out the truth, if we carry on our enquiry with reasonable care ; for Christ, in providing us with the means of knowing what He taught, must have made that means sufficiently conspicuous, so that men may be able to recognise it without much difficulty.

To state in a few words the various opinions to be discussed. Some tell us that the Bible, and the Bible alone, is the means Christ has appointed to lead men to the full knowledge of His doctrine. Others say that He has appointed this sacred work, together with an immediate light and motion of the Holy Ghost, communicated to the individual. Others again who read it maintain that He means us to read the New Testament, but to complete and interpret it with the writings of the Early Fathers. Many think that we should avail ourselves of every possible source of information, even outside the Bible and the Fathers, or simply accept on His doctrine what is given as such by men who have made these researches. Catholics assert that Christ has appointed for all, for the learned as well as the illiterate, an infallible teaching authority under one infallible head. A few non-Catholic divines accept and defend this opinion " minus the infallible head ; " others even do away with the infallibility of the teaching staff as a body, and are satisfied with " authorised teachers."

These being practically the only opinions advanced after the lapse of nineteen hundred years, it is evident that one or other of them must be right : Christ could not be said to have given us the means of knowing His doctrine if after nineteen centuries they had not yet been discovered by men.

Test to judge them.

In order to find out which of those means is the one appointed by Christ, we may perhaps feel inclined to think that the best and only safe plan is to consult history. Unfortunately, all men do not understand it in the same way ; and so, although we intend to consult it, we are not sure that it is the best way to convince the reader. Therefore we prefer taking a common-sense argument as the basis of our enquiry, and assert that the means appointed by Christ must from its very nature, suffice to bring about the result He has in view, and that any means which from its very nature cannot do so, must be discarded.

We do not say that a means should be discarded from the mere fact that men, though offered it, do not actually arrive at the knowledge of Christ's doctrine : their failure in this matter may not be due to the nature of the instrument, but rather to the want of good will, or intelligence, on their part. All we insist upon is that any means should be discarded which, when used by a man of average intelligence and good will, does not attain the result Christ has in view.

Neither do we say that a means should be passed over because it cannot come within the reach of all men in a short time, and so spread everywhere, within a few weeks, our Saviour's teaching. It would indeed be absurd to hold that no means can, of its very nature, enable men to know Christ's doctrine, if it is not a sort of divining wand, pointing out, not only the truth, but even lands hitherto unknown. All we again say is that the means in question must be able to reach, after a reasonable time, the different countries that may happen to be discovered, and then enable the inhabitants of those countries to know the teaching of Christ and to have one and the same faith with the rest of the known world. Now to apply our test.

I.—The New Testament alone is not the Means.

1. Is the New Testament alone the means appointed by Christ ? Even before applying our test, we may *anticipate* and give *a negative answer* to the question, from the fact that Christ did not Himself write the book and hand it over to the Apostles, with a commission to make as many copies of it as possible and spread them amongst men. And not only did He not write Himself, but no mention is even made in the New Testament of a commission to write given by Him to His Apostles. On the contrary, those of them who write are few : even St. John, " the beloved disciple," who would certainly be most anxious to comply faithfully and promptly with every wish of his Divine Master, put off the writing of his Gospel till the end of the first century. Had Christ intended the New Testament to be the only or chief means of

spreading His doctrine, we could not account for all this; while there is nothing to be wondered at, if He let His Apostles free to choose that means, without making it the only or chief one of propagating His teaching.

2. But if we apply the test above mentioned, it becomes evident that He could not have appointed the New Testament as the only or chief instrument to procure the end He had in view ; because its very nature makes it *absolutely powerless* to enable men to know His doctrine and to be certain and all of one mind about its tenets, the very object He wishes to attain. The New Testament, we say, is absolutely powerless in this matter, because, if we are given nothing but that Book,—and, in this opinion, Christ is supposed to have appointed nothing else to enable us to know His teaching,— we are at once stopped by this question, which cannot be settled by the Bible : May I trust the writers of this Book ? We hold that this question cannot be settled by the Bible ; for to quote it in this connection would be to take for granted that we can safely trust the writers, believe what they say, and be sure that their apparent simplicity is not meant to gain the reader's confidence and deceive him the more easily. It is a common saying that a man cannot be a witness in his own cause.

There is another question to be answered : before we can be certain that we know where to find Christ's doctrine, we have not only to make sure that the writers of the book called the New Testament, which was composed eighteen hundred years ago, are trustworthy ; we must also be certain that we possess a genuine copy or translation of their work.—Now, to settle this point, we cannot appeal to the copy we have in our hands, as to do so would be taking for granted what has precisely to be proved, viz., that our copy, with its several parts, is the genuine and unaltered work of those writers we have spoken of.—Therefore, in addition to the New Testament itself, Christ must have given us, over and above, some means by which we may know for certain that the writers of the Book are trustworthy and that we have a genuine copy or translation of the original work.

3. But these are only preliminary objections to this theory. As a matter of fact, even if the trustworthiness of its writers and the genuineness of the copy or translation we possess were beyond question, Christ could not have

appointed the New Testament as the only means through which we are to know His teaching, be sure of its tenets and be all of one mind about them, because

A. The New Testament *does not contain the whole* doctrine of Christ. Of this we have the positive assurance of the Holy Writers themselves. St. John says: "Many other signs also did Jesus, in the sight of His disciples, which are not written in this Book" (John xx. 30). "There are also many other things which Jesus did, which, if they were written every one, the world itself, I think, would not be able to contain the books that should be written" (John xxi. 25). These words do not uphold, but, on the contrary, clearly go against, the opinion that all Christ did and said is contained in one volume of limited dimensions. St. Paul also implies that he himself did not write down all he taught, when he makes a distinction between his writings and his oral instructions: "Hold the traditions which you have learned whether by word or by our epistle" (2 Thess. ii. 14); "The things that thou hast heard from me before many witnesses, the same commend to faithful men who shall be fit to teach others also" (2 Tim. ii. 2). St. John makes the same distinction: "Having more things to write to you, I would not by paper and ink, for I hope that I shall be with you, and speak face to face, that your joy may be full" (2 John i. 12). From the New Testament we learn that the Bible does not contain the whole teaching of Christ, nor that of the Apostles, who are sent by our Divine Lord expressly to make known all things whatsoever He has commanded them.

B. Can those who will accept nothing but the Bible feel sure that the New Testament comprises at least the *chief points* of Christ's teaching? No, for this is a question about which it is silent. Consequently, to prove and justify their contention that, by taking what is in the Scriptures, they know at least the chief points of Christ's doctrine and therefore enough to be saved, they are bound both by reason and by our Lord Himself to seek evidence outside the Bible. This again shows the unsoundness of their principle, "The Bible, and nothing but the Bible." If they do not wish to make this research, we declare they have no grounds to believe and say that Holy Scripture contains all that is necessary for salvation; and therefore they rashly expose themselves to the danger of not believing what is requisite to be saved; God and reason must condemn such temerity.

C. The New Testament, on the supposition that we may safely accept the testimony of its writers, does not establish even the *essential* points. If we are to stand by the Bible alone, we cannot even know *which books* form part of it. We said above that we cannot appeal to the Scriptures themselves to settle this difficulty; but, even if we did so, we should get no answer.—It is also essential that we should be in possession of the exact *meaning* of the words of Christ, as it could not otherwise be said that we know the doctrine He imparted to the world. Now the Bible seldom explains what our Lord meant, though, judging from the contradictory interpretations of His words (see pp. 37-39), they are sometimes difficult to understand.

Only two passages of the New Testament might justify the theory we are considering; but they prove nothing in its favour, if the context is, as it should be, used to explain their meaning. St. John says: "These are written that you may believe that Jesus is the Son of God, and that believing you may have life in His Name" (John xx. 31). But from this we can only conclude that we have enough text to convince us of the divinity of Christ, and enable us to find out from the Bible or *elsewhere* all that we have to believe; we cannot infer that we shall find therein everything that Christ taught. Our Lord says to the Jews: "Search the Scriptures" (John v. 39); but He did not add that, in doing so, they would find either His whole doctrine, or its chief points; indeed, He could not have added this, for He was referring not to the New Testament, but to the Old, which surely does not contain His teaching.

D. Even if it comprised the whole doctrine ever taught by Christ, or if we were convinced from other authorities—the inspired writers being silent on that point—that it contains at least its chief points, would it follow that the New Testament could then procure the end Christ had in view? No, for we must remember He wishes *all men* to know His teaching; and therefore the means appointed for that end must be of such a character as to place it within their reach. It is clear that, of all means, a book is the last Christ would have chosen, nineteen centuries ago, for that purpose; and it is not likely to be the instrument He would choose even for men of the present day.

It is a well known fact that the Bible, even the New Testament, was out of the reach of most men before the invention of printing, so that, even granting that the majority in those days were able to read,—which is very doubtful—they had very little chance of ever studying that book: yet, if Christ intends it to be the only means of spreading His doctrine, He expects men to have and read it.—This He expects, not only of men who lived before the invention of printing, but of the numberless modern tribes into whose various tongues the New Testament has not even yet been translated. Must we then say that He also expects and obliges them to learn a foreign language in order to be able to read the Bible?

Even though the New Testament were translated into all languages and given to every one, it would not yet follow that all men would thus practically be enabled to know Christ's teaching; for many cannot read.—And as to those who can, much would depend whether the text or translation they use is correct. It cannot be truly said that any one knows the doctrine taught by our Lord, if he has studied only a spurious text, or one of which the genuineness is doubtful. It is very strange, if Christ meant the New Testament to be the only source from which we are to draw the exact knowledge of what He taught, that He has allowed the original text of the Book to disappear, and that, with regard to copies, not to speak of translations, He has allowed the copyists to make numberless blunders. Mill (✠ 1707) at the beginning of last century could point out thirty thousand different readings in the manuscripts of the New Testament, and in our days biblical scholars speak of a hundred thousand, when they include the different readings found in the early translations or quotations made by the Fathers. This being the case, is it true to say that every one who has a Bible is really enabled to find out what Christ taught? And can a man aware of the existence of that multitude of different readings feel sure that, by perusing his own copy of the New Testament, he will certainly know the pure teaching of Christ? It seems to us that every one is bound to doubt it, so long as he has not compared those different readings (a thing which our Lord cannot expect ordinary readers and busy men to do), or so long as he has not some authority besides his Bible to convince him that his New Testament gives the substance of Christ's doctrine. Consequently, if men have nothing but their copy of the Bible as the means of knowing what our Saviour taught, they cannot practically arrive at that *certainty of mind* which is implied in all knowledge worth the name.

But we go a step further, and say that, even if they were sure of the possession of a genuine copy or correct translation of the New Testament, they would not, even then, be able to know what Christ taught so as to be certain and unanimous in their belief. Few, if any, could overcome the difficulty of *rightly understanding* what they read. This is clear in the case of the minority who might wish to peruse the original text in Hebrew, Greek or Latin; as no one can rightly comprehend the New Testament in the original tongue, unless he be well versed not only in Theology and Exegesis, but also in languages, and know the meaning which the people, living at the time its books were composed, attached to its words and expressions. This alone implies, not only the knowledge of a dictionary, but that of the customs, habits, manners, history, relations to other countries, trade, etc., of the peoples mentioned in those different books.—Nearly the same difficulties would be met by those who could read the New Testament only in a translation, however correct. For they also would have to be sound critics and theologians to avoid being misled by apparent contradictions, obscure passages, and strange expressions; otherwise they could not feel certain that they know what Christ taught.—As a matter of fact St. Peter tells us that the Scriptures are sometimes difficult to understand, and were actually taken in a wrong sense even by those who lived in the Apostles' time; he mentions that, in the writings of St. Paul, there are "some things hard to be understood, which the unlearned and unstable wrest, as also the other Scriptures, to their own perdition" (2 Peter iii. 16). And just as the Hebrew, Greek or Latin text has been misinterpreted, even what is called an "authorised version" has been misconstrued over and over again. History tells us that heretics have always based their errors on the Bible; and, in our days, contradictory meanings are given to the same text by the several Christian sects among which we live. For example, the texts, "The Father is greater than I" (John xiv. 28), "This is My body" (Matt. xxvi. 26), "Thou art Peter, and upon this rock I will build My Church" (Matt. xvi. 18), "God will have all men to be saved" (1 Tim. ii. 4), are all interpreted in contradictory ways. According to some, the words "It behoveth a bishop to be . . . the husband of one wife" (1 Tim. iii. 2) imply that bishops should be married men; according to others, "They should not have been married more than once," or even, "They should have only one wife at a time." Now it is clear that, if one of the meanings attached to a text is the right one, all the others that are in contradiction to it, are wrong; and, consequently, there must be some difficulty in understanding that passage since some misunderstand it.—Speaking of the Bible in general, Luther says: "It is impossible to fathom the Scriptures; we can only skip over their surface; to understand their sense would be a wonder."[1] "In Scripture there are more things unknown than known to me," writes St. Augustine (St. Aug. Epist. ad Jan.) Yet, if the opinion we are considering be true, Christ offers men the Bible as their only means of knowing His doctrine, of being certain about its tenets, and of possessing one and the same faith. No, since Christ wishes such an end to be attained, He has not, and cannot have, chosen the New Testament as the only or chief means of putting it within the reach of all: even now a genuine copy or translation of the Book is for some people difficult to procure; a New Testament was a rare book before the invention of printing, and, above all, the subtleties of interpretation are such that they naturally lead even earnest and learned men to misunderstand or doubt the meaning of a text, and, as a consequence, must produce uncertainty in the mind and cause division in the faith. In short, Christ has not and cannot have chosen the New Testament as the only or chief way of knowing His doctrine, because, of its very nature, that way cannot attain the end He had in view.

E. As a matter of fact, the *early Christians* did not stand by the Bible alone, but must have accepted information from other sources. For they did not find in the New Testament that Baptism given by heretics was valid, or that Sunday was to be kept holy instead of Saturday, or that it was lawful to eat blood or things strangled, or that young children were to

[1] Audin, Life of Luther, bk. II.

be baptised. If we judge *modern Christians* by their deeds, we question whether any of them believe that they should be guided by the Bible only; for they also keep holy the Sunday instead of the Sabbath, they do on the Sunday things which the Old Testament forbids, and which the New Testament does not make lawful, such as lighting fires (Exod. xxxv. 3); they baptise young children, though our Lord seems to say that men should first believe and then be baptised (Matt. xxviii. 9); they do not abstain from things strangled and blood, though this is distinctly commanded by the Apostles (Acts xv. 20). How do they know that they are not going against our Lord's commands or wishes, since the Bible seems to condemn them? Because, in practice, they do not, any more than the early Christians, look upon the Bible as their only guide; and they are right, for Christ never meant that men should do so.

II.—The New Testament, even with an interior light and motion of the Holy Ghost, is not the means.

Is the New Testament, together with a supernatural light from the Holy Ghost, the means appointed by Christ for men to know His doctrine?

1. First of all, it cannot be, for even if the Holy Ghost enlighten every reader of the New Testament, it still remains true that the Book does not contain the *whole* of Christ's teaching.

2. That the Holy Ghost could, in His infinite goodness, enable every reader of the New Testament rightly to understand its sense, there is no doubt; but that He does so is another question. We admit that He may and does guide some, so that they derive a real benefit for their souls from the reading of the Bible; we even admit that He helps them, to a certain extent, to understand, and, through the virtue of faith, to make an act of supernatural belief in what Christ taught; but the fact to which we have just alluded, that different and even contradictory meanings are given to the same text by earnest readers, shows clearly the unsoundness of the opinion that the Holy Ghost Himself guides and enlightens *every one* who reads the sacred Word. He certainly could not lead a man to understand a given text in an heretical

sense—make him conclude, for example, as some have done, that Christ does not know everything, from the fact that we read in the Bible that He cannot point out the day of the Last Judgment (Mark xiii. 32); nor could He lead men to give contradictory meanings to the same text, making one, for instance, understand that the words "This is My Body" mean "This is no bread, but truly and really the Flesh and Blood of Christ," and make another understand the opposite, viz., "This is only bread, and not the Flesh and Blood of Christ."

3. History proves that even pious readers who believe that the Holy Ghost makes them understand the Bible, give such contradictory meanings to the same text, as and this clearly shows that even amongst them some are under a *delusion*.

4. Now, why so, if not because we have *no test* to make sure that the Holy Ghost speaks to us? If there exists no such test, men can never be certain that what they hear is from above.

III.—The New Testament, even together with the writings of the Early Fathers, is not the means.

It is so evident that men cannot be sure of Christ's teaching and arrive at unity of faith, if they have nothing but the Bible, that even those who, in theory, admit nothing but the the Holy Writings, have, in practice, recourse to other sources of information, not only to find out which books should be accepted under the name of the New Testament, but also to understand them rightly. Many even regret that theory openly and assert that, together with the New Testament, Christ has given us the writings of the early Fathers to interpret it and solve all other difficulties which may arise about the genuineness of certain passages, or even of the Books themselves. They say that the Fathers had ways to find out whether a certain book or letter was the work of an inspired writer, or merely apocryphal; that living nearer, as they did, to the Apostles than we do, they had every facility to know what sense the sacred writers attached to certain passages in their works: they insist that the early Fathers are the only safe interpreters of the New Testament, and that, although Christ did not actually mention them any more than the Holy Scriptures,

He undoubtedly means us to study their works, as well as the New Testament, that we may know His teaching.

Now, what are we to think of this theory? We admit that it is profitable to consult the early Fathers, if only for the sake of the wisdom and knowledge displayed in their writings; we grant that, living nearer to the time of the Apostles, they had better opportunities of knowing what they taught; we even grant that their opinion must be of supreme moment, whenever they all interpret, in one and the same manner, any text of the Bible, as pertaining to the doctrine of faith and morals (see Encyc. Providentissimus Deus, authorised translat. pp. 17, 18). We do not however think that Christ intended them, together with the New Testament, to be the only or chief means for men to know His doctrine, because (and here we again apply our test) that means could not bring about the result He had in view.

1. If it is only through the Bible and the early Fathers that we can know it, then it follows that *all men* must procure the Fathers' writings; and they are surely far more difficult of access than a New Testament. They must, besides, make sure that the copy they are in possession of is genuine; for the heretics of the first centuries at times altered the writings of the Fathers; and this alone may entail long and tedious comparison of texts. Again, they must acquire the requisite knowledge of languages, Latin, Greek, Syriac, in order to understand these works; this also implies long study; if they prefer reading a *translation*, they have to make sure, as best they can, that the translator was qualified for his work and was possessed of an orthodox copy of the original; two points which it is not easy to decide, but which must be settled before a translation may be trusted. When they have become versed in the languages used by the Fathers, or have secured a correct translation of their writings, they must read all that the principal Fathers have written, before they are able to decide what opinion may be said to be theirs; as an insight into their writings will at once disclose the fact that they sometimes disagree and even contradict one another. Now, of the one hundred and fifty quarto volumes published by Migne called "Bibliotheca Patrum," St. Jerome alone takes up nine, St. Augustine sixteen, St. Gregory the Great five, St. Chrysostom eighteen, St. Cyril of Alexandria ten (the two last named being published in Greek and Latin), and so on. Are we then

to say that Christ intends and expects every man to go through this vast work? Evidently not. 2. But, even granting that every one could do so, would the labour entailed bring about the result our Lord has in view? No; for those who read the Fathers *disagree* even as to what is and what is not Christ's teaching on most important points of doctrine: compare, for instance, Dr. Moorhouse's and Father B. Vaughan's lectures in Manchester in 1895. This speaks for itself and shows that, if Christ has given us only the writings of the Fathers and the Bible to arrive at the knowledge of His doctrine, He has chosen a means to which only a few can have recourse, and which does not enable even those few to know His teaching so as to be unanimous about and convinced of its tenets.

Therefore such a means cannot be the one appointed by Christ to attain the end He had in view, any more than the Bible alone or together with an interior illumination of the Holy Ghost.

CHAPTER IV.

THE MEANS THAT REASON TELLS US CHRIST MUST HAVE APPOINTED, SINCE HE WISHES MEN TO ARRIVE AT A REAL KNOWLEDGE OF HIS TEACHING.

I.—Christ must have intended that men should be taught by their fellow men.

1. Not one of the means we have considered in the last chapter can be that appointed by Christ to attain the end He has in view, as not one of them can enable men to know His teaching, be certain of its tenets, and be all of one and the same mind about it. Therefore it must follow that Christ intends men to be taught His doctrine by their fellow men; for the human mind cannot suggest any *other way* to attain the end proposed; and there is little likelihood that Christ appointed a means the existence and nature of which have not even been suspected after nineteen centuries.

2. There seems to be *every reason* why Christ should have appointed the means we now consider; for man naturally accepts the authority of a teacher, and easily believes what he is taught; almost all the knowledge he possesses has been imparted to him by teachers, and this is particularly true of religious knowledge; even in those Christian denominations which, in theory, will have nothing but the Bible, we see two classes of people, the masters and the disciples, the former explaining the meaning of the Scriptures and binding the latter to accept their teaching as a condition of belonging to their denomination.

3. This is the only possible means of bringing Christ's doctrine *within reach of all*, and especially of those who cannot read or have no great power for intellectual work. Hence, we hold that Christ must have intended men to be taught His religion by their fellow men. But whom does He mean to be the teachers? Does He permit any one

to impart His doctrine to others, or does He allow only a certain class of men to undertake this work?

II.—He must have authorised a certain body of men as Teachers, and made His authorisation manifest to the world.

It is evident that our Lord cannot allow everybody to constitute himself a teacher. If He wishes us to be taught His religion and have the same belief, reason demands that He should give us *competent* masters: the incompetent cannot possibly impart a doctrine of which they are themselves ignorant.—However this will not suffice. We may be addressed by various teachers. Unless we can decide which of them are qualified, we may be taught anything but the pure Gospel. Our Lord must consequently have provided us with the *means to discern the competent from the incompetent*.

But even then we may find the doctrine set forth as Christ's religion unpalatable and refuse to hear those we consider to be qualified. If Christ wishes us to listen to them, He must make His desire manifest and even give us sufficient grounds to conclude that we are *not free to reject* their teaching, distasteful though it may be.

To express these three conditions differently: if our Lord wishes us to know His doctrine and not to be misled by incompetent masters, He must authorise a certain body of men as teachers and enable us to discern them from all others. His authorising them will be a guarantee that they are competent and trustworthy and a proof that He wishes and even binds us to listen to them. He may not oblige us to listen to one rather than to the other; but we are not free to reject them all, once we know that they hold from above a right to teach, as that right implies for us a duty to accept their doctrine.

If it is so important that we should listen to none but those whom Christ wishes us to hear, it is absolutely necessary to know what kind of evidence should be considered as a conclusive proof that a particular teacher or body of teachers are authorised by Him. Many hold that He tacitly and implicitly authorises all such as have made His religion their special study; others limit His authorisation to those who have been approved by a body of learned, honest, and faithful men, or even by one man who can be depended upon; others again hold that none but orthodox teachers should be looked upon as authorised by our Lord. Can reason accept any of these guarantees as a conclusive proof that a teacher is authorised by Him?

A. The fact that a man has studied His religion is not a sufficient proof that he is authorised by Christ.

The supporters of the first opinion tell us, that the only way to acquire a knowledge of past events is to consult historical documents, to hunt up every available field of information, to listen to men who are supposed to have already acquired that knowledge, and to take for granted that their views are correct, so long as they are not proved erroneous. Now, they say, as Christ taught hundreds of years ago, He undoubtedly means us to treat His teaching as a past event, and therefore authorises those who have spent their time in seeking His doctrine to impart their knowledge to others. Consequently, we may truly say that He gives the Bible, the writings of the Fathers and all other sources of information to those who have the taste, the time, the capacity, for study, and authorises any man who has studied His religion, to impart his knowledge of it to his fellow men: which means that any man who has studied Christ's religion, is practically authorised by Him to teach it.

To our mind, this opinion is *playing on the word* "authorised." Those who have studied are "authorised" to impart their knowledge, in the sense that they are, to a certain extent, able and free to do so: but it does not follow that they are "authorised," in the sense that "they have received from Christ authority" to impart it,—in other words, that Christ wishes or binds men to listen to them. For, if He did, He would make it impossible for many to know what He Himself taught, and consequently for all men to be united in the same faith.—Scholars and teachers are liable, not to say, certain, to differ, and even to fall into error. If we take into account that there are often different ways of interpreting a text and of reading a document, and that arguments which convince one man often fail to convince another, we can hardly expect all to agree; if, besides, we consider that the documents to be studied are numerous, and that, as a consequence, every scholar not being able to study all for himself must depend for a knowledge of what they contain upon other scholars, who in turn may and must have relied on others and perhaps on worthless authorities, we cannot expect that men who have studied different documents and consulted different authorities, will often come to the same conclusion. Besides, scholars themselves have preconceived ideas, the result of their early training, associations, and surroundings, which are not easily shaken off; taking human nature as it is, they also may form a rash opinion, and make mistakes. Therefore, we may be sure, on many points they will *hold different views*, and even then being aware that others do not agree with them, they will seldom feel certain that they have found out the truth, and that what they believe to be Christ's doctrine, will not, after further researches and discussions, turn out to be a mere human opinion. The same divisions will naturally be found amongst the teachers trained by them; nay more, the latter being less deeply read, will sometimes think themselves competent to form an opinion of their own, different from that of the writers they consult. Naturally, if the scholars and teachers are divided, the disciples will be so too; with the result that if some do know what Christ taught, the others will not, and being unable to decide which teacher is right, will never be able to arrive at certitude. We may therefore expect to find in a large city as many independent churches and chapels as there are opinions as to what Christ taught, wished, approved, or would approve if He were still on earth. We may even be prepared for another result: some men, whether scholars or not, will soon, if they happen to go from one teacher or professor to another, notice those differences, and will begin to doubt whether any are right, or at any rate will feel convinced that, just as it is certain that Christ intended all men to know His doctrine, be sure of its tenets, and have one and the same faith, so also it is clear that He omitted to appoint a means of procuring that end, if He gives the same right to all those teachers differing amongst themselves, to spread His doctrine: in other words, a certain number of men will call in question, or deny, Christ's infinite wisdom, and, being consistent, will fall, not only into indifference, but into *infidelity*. Now a system that leads men to *divisions* in the faith, to *doubt, blasphemy* and even *infidelity*, is already judged, and cannot be the one chosen by Christ. We need not consequently ask if the system we have been considering does, as a fact, bring about the result Christ has in view: its very nature makes it impossible.

But if there be still the least doubt in the reader's mind about its actual efficacy, *facts* are at hand to prove that the results are exactly what we have anticipated. Scholars and teachers and their adherents are divided on most important and practical points of doctrine. The school of "Higher Criticism" denies almost everything which others look upon as undeniable; even the Divinity of Christ and His very existence have become for some of them an open question; in their eyes, the New Testament is no longer a trustworthy historical document, but a book of legends; and this their view is accepted, if not publicly taught, in some of our Universities. Others, who still reject this fundamental theory, and believe in the existence and Divinity of Christ, are divided on such an important point as the immortality of the soul: Mr. Petavel-Olleff, in "L'Immortalité Conditionnelle," quotes texts from the Bible to show that for the wicked and those who prefer annihilation, there is no after-life; annihilation, writes Dr. Freer, is the grim lot of those who do not possess faith in Christ; and, in this, he has the approbation of Mr. Gladstone, if we may believe "The Expository Times" (July, 1896, p. 433). Others, admitting the immortality of the soul, do not agree as to what becomes of it after death. The United Brethren believe in eternal punishment, and the Universalists in the salvation of all men (cf. Chambers's Encyc. edit. 1895); the Rev. Vernon Staley, in his "Catholic Religion," a catechism much in favour with the High Church party, rejects the opinion of those who hold that the innocent soul goes at once to Heaven, while the soul of the wicked goes at once to Hell, and tells us (p. 181) that before the resurrection the good do not go to Heaven (martyrs alone being excepted), nor the wicked to Hell; as to the fate of those who are neither wicked enough to go to Hell, nor pure enough to go to Heaven, some send them straight to Heaven, others hold that they wait in a place of suffering, until they are purified. Some teach that it is useless to pray for the dead; others (Vernon Staley, loc. cit. 213) invite us to intercede even for the damned. The majority of Churches believe in the resurrection of all men; but Christadelphians (Chambers's Enc.) admit that of the good only; and Swedenborgians (ibid.) deny altogether the resurrection of the material body. Catholics, Orthodox Greeks, and some High Church people, maintain that God is honoured when we ask His Saints, and especially the Blessed Virgin Mary, to pray for us; others condemn this practice, as against Scripture and reason. One school teaches that a priest can forgive the sins of the repentant sinner ; another denies that Christ ever gave such a power to men. In one church we are told that a priest can change bread and wine into the Body and Blood of Christ; in another we hear that the bread remains bread, but contains the Body of our Lord ; while in a third we are informed that Christ's Body is only in Heaven, and nowhere else. The Lutheran says that Baptism is necessary for salvation ; Methodists (ibid.) hold the reverse ; and Baptists (ibid.) admit its necessity only for adults. The Plymouth Brethren (ibid.) deny the office of the ministry—any of their male members may preach ; the Ranters (ibid.) allow even women to preach ; while most denominations require a regular appointment for their ministers. Anglican divines are divided as to what the powers of the Priesthood are : some hold that a priest has power to cause that Christ may be really present in the Holy Eucharist, and thereby to offer a Sacrifice, and also power to forgive sins with a judgment ratified in Heaven ; and others deny that a priest has such a power : in their eyes, a priest is a man who can celebrate the Lord's Supper, declare officially the forgiveness of sins, and preach the Gospel—a view which is supported by many outside their own denomination. But even those who believe that a priest can forgive sins, do not agree about the necessity of confessing them to him. The Rev. Vernon Staley tells us that confession is not necessary for forgiveness (loc. cit. 352), though this is hardly reconcilable with what he writes on page 362, about the necessity of confessing every sin if one goes to confession ; Catholic and Orthodox Greeks hold that all grievous sins must be confessed, whenever it is possible, if one wish to be forgiven, while there is no necessity for confessing smaller faults. Some admit as God's word several books of the Old and New Testament which others reject completely as apocryphal, or consider as merely pious, but not as inspired books. We could continue this list of contradictions; but we think we have said enough to show that there exist divisions on most important matters of belief among the various Christian denominations. However, though for one reason or another these sects have become very numerous, we do not say that the 293 which, according to Whittaker's Almanack (1897), are to be found in England and Wales, differ from one another on doctrinal points, or that they might not possibly, as far as doctrine is concerned, be grouped into five or six different categories; but three things are certain: (1) they do not all teach the same doctrine; (2) the Catholic Church disagrees with them all in matters of faith; (3) some hold many erroneous views, and consequently do not know what Christ taught; for if one view be correct, another in contradiction to it must be erroneous, as Christ made no contradictory statements.

Now, as this state of affairs is brought about by the teachers, it is evident that Christ cannot intend that men should listen to every one who may have studied His religion, as this would be equivalent to His willing the end—unity of faith—whilst He makes it impossible by giving to those who teach contrary opinions an equal right to be heard.

B. The fact that a man is authorised by apparently learned and honest judges is not a proof that he is authorised by Christ.

The second opinion is liable to the same objection; for those very teachers who give expression to opposite views are, for the most part, authorised by men supposed to be learned, honest, and competent judges. This evidently shows that the intention of Christ cannot be that mankind should listen to every teacher that may be authorised by judges apparently qualified, since He wishes all men to know one and the same doctrine, and have one and the same faith.

C. The fact that a man is an orthodox teacher, is not a proof that he is authorised by Christ.

Shall we say, with the third opinion, that orthodox teachers are undoubtedly authorised by Christ, and should therefore be listened to in preference to others? This would certainly make it more easy to attain the end Christ has in view. But where is *the test* by which we may find them out? The two opinions we have just been discussing claim to give us that test; this third seems to leave us free to decide for ourselves: and it is a strange system that supposes that those who come to be taught are to be the judges of the teachers themselves! How can ignorant people—how can Pagans, decide whether their master teaches the pure doctrine of Christ?

Evidently, our Saviour must have given us some other means of knowing whether a teacher, or a given body of teachers, are truly authorised by Him, as otherwise we should have to conclude that He wishes us to receive the doctrine of certain authorised teachers, but has given us no means of ascertaining who they are,—a state of things which we cannot reconcile with His wisdom.

D. The following would be a conclusive proof that a particular teacher is authorised by Christ.

To our mind, the question would be solved if every teacher were directly pointed out by Christ Himself, or enabled, in confirmation of His mission, to work wonders which no one without God's special help could perform; or again, if such a teacher were appointed by men who could, by the wonderful works they performed, show that the Almighty ratified and confirmed what they had done or said; or, in the third place, if he could prove that he was the legitimate successor of men undoubtedly authorised by Christ; although, in the two latter cases, it would be necessary to show that such authority has not been withdrawn. No one could doubt that such a teacher is authorised by Christ; consequently, *unless* some other means equally sufficient and satisfactory can be suggested, we hold that Christ must have appointed one of these, as a conclusive proof that a particular teacher, or body of teachers, is authorised by Him.

III.—He must preserve the teachers as a body from teaching error.

1. We add that the authorised teachers should be infallible as a body; for otherwise the end Christ has in view might not be attained. If they are not infallible as a body, they are then, like all other teachers, liable to error; like them, they may interpret the Bible incorrectly, read their own fancies into the Fathers, misunderstand tradition and the general

consent of past teachers on a given point, and build up a
sophistical argument; like other leaders of thought, they may
wish to be original, and thus be induced to lay down rash or
erroneous propositions; they may import their religious knowledge from Germany, from Universities in which the pure
Gospel of Christ is no longer taught, with the result that the
teachers formed by such professors—nay, all the teachers of a
given country—may be misled and fall into error; and as what
takes place in one nation may take place in another, it is quite
possible that, after a certain length of time, the teaching of
Christ may be entirely superseded by views merely human and
rationalistic. Indeed we see every reason why this should
happen, for it is not so easy and natural to arrive at the
truth and agree in religious matters, as it is in matters
capable of mathematical demonstration. But if it is possible
that *all teachers* should *fall into error* on one or more points of
doctrine, this possibility alone implies that Christ has not
taken the necessary means to secure that men should know
His teaching. But as Christ has undoubtedly adopted the
means of obtaining the end He had in view, we must conclude
that He has made it impossible that His authorised teachers
should, as a body, propound error.

IV.—He must have placed some supreme au-
thority over the teachers and the taught.

But, if the authorised teachers are as a body infallible, can
we say that Christ has done all that was absolutely necessary
to bring about and maintain that unity of faith which must
exist among men who receive the same teaching? No, for
this does not imply that a certain number of *individual
teachers* will not fall into error, mislead their hearers, and
thus cause division in the faith. We say, therefore, that if
Christ wishes men to know what He taught, and to have one
and the same faith, He must have either made every one
infallible—and facts prove that He has not—or instituted
a ready *check upon the teaching and spreading of error*, a prompt
remedy to divisions in the faith, and even a ready solution to
possible doubts. For, as is evident, if a certain number of
men, and above all if whole generations were condemned to
ignorance of the truth, through want of a ready means of
ascertaining it or of checking the spreading of falsehood, we

should be justified in saying that Christ willed the end, but did not will the means.

Reason tells us that the teaching of an erroneous doctrine cannot be prevented unless Christ has established some authority which each one of the teachers, as well as of the taught, is bound to obey, and without whose permission no one may act as minister of the Gospel. While, if there existed such an authority over every district or country, we should have in it the practical check we required, as every teacher whose doctrine appeared unsound could be easily denied all authority to preach, or deprived of such, and, should he refuse to submit to that decision, the faithful could be forbidden to listen to him. Hence we hold that Christ must have placed some supreme authority over the teachers and the taught.

V.—He must, in certain cases, preserve that supreme authority from teaching error.

However, we are not sure that the injunctions of that authority will always be obeyed. For the fact that a man and his doctrine are condemned does not imply that the doctrine is false; and if, in spite of its being condemned, it may nevertheless be true, it is quite possible that many may think themselves justified in still believing it,—just as the first Christians were justified in believing the doctrine taught by the Apostles, though it was condemned by the apparently lawful authority ruling in Jerusalem; or as the Roman Cardinals were justified in believing in the rotation of the earth, though Galileo had been forbidden to teach that opinion; or as certain Anglicans think they are justified in believing in the use of prayer for the dead, though the doctrine of Purgatory has been condemned by the authorities of their Church. Now, if a doctrine, though condemned by a lawful superior, may after all be *true*, there is no doubt that, if it is true, it may be rightly *retained* and *believed*, and, so long as the subject does not teach it to others, the superior can make no objection. Moreover, if it may be rightly retained and believed, it is almost certain to be *taught*. But since a condemnation is no conclusive proof against the orthodoxy of a doctrine, there is no doubt that even false doctrines, though condemned, may and will be believed and most probably taught; and if so, it is evident that, in spite of the injunctions of a lawful authority, there may and will be *divisions in the faith*, and most likely even in the teaching. Now, how can these divisions be prevented?

To our mind, unity of faith cannot be maintained, unless that authority may not only condemn false doctrines and point out the truth, but also *bind* the teachers, as well as the taught, *to believe* that a certain doctrine is false, and another true or the doctrine taught by Christ. If our Lord gives such a right to that authority, then He virtually binds men to believe what that authority teaches, and eventually to give up their own way of interpreting the Bible and the Fathers; they must not only cease teaching a condemned doctrine, but interiorly believe it to be false and, consequently, unsupported by, or contrary to, the Scriptures. We do not say that this is sure to do away with divisions in the faith, as men may choose to resist authority; it certainly makes unity of belief possible.

But, as is evident, if Christ bind everybody to believe one doctrine to be false simply because it has been condemned by a certain authority, and another to be true because it is declared to be so by that same authority, it follows that in such cases as the one here described, He must grant that authority a privilege of immunity from error; for *Christ could not bind a man to believe what is false.*

VI.—He must have granted that supreme authority to one man.

One point remains to be settled: Who should constitute that infallible authority? Should it be one man or several?

The fact that it must afford a prompt check to the spread of error, and a speedy solution to doubts on points of doctrine, leads us to assert that the infallible authority in question cannot be a General Council of all the teachers in the world, or even of the head teachers.

1. It cannot be vested in a General Council.

If we grant that the Council's decision would be infallible and final as given by the teachers as a body—we have just said that the teachers as a body must be infallible—there would be in the present state of our religious divisions an almost insurmountable difficulty in getting a decision which all would feel bound to consider as infallible and final.

Let us suppose, for example, that the members of one of the three hundred denominations in the British Isles, or the heads and chief representatives of ten of those denominations, convinced that truth must be one, and finding that what one Church accepts and believes as Christ's doctrine is denied and rejected by another, wish to know what Christ did really teach. Let us further imagine that they hold as certain that only a General Council can give a satisfactory answer to their enquiries. How can this be secured? There is undoubtedly no such meeting sitting at present; therefore, according to this opinion, there is no means of dispelling doubt and arriving at certainty, except trying to induce the various teachers to assemble and hold a General Synod.[1] But before this can be accomplished, one point has to be settled, viz., who should and who should not be invited to it. Should Unitarians, who deny the divinity of Christ, though they claim to follow His teaching, be summoned? Should an appeal be made to the heads of all the various Christian denominations? Nay, even to all the teachers of all Christian denominations? For unless this question be settled, nobody could feel sure that the Council was a general one, and, therefore, able to render an infallible and final decision on any point of doctrine. Indeed, for this very reason, the question must be decided so as to leave no room for uncertainty; but if to do away with all doubts an infallible decision should be required, who is to give it, since a General Council only is infallible? Christ has left us in an inextricable difficulty, if He has not settled the point Himself, or if it has not already been decided by such an assembly. But granting that it has been settled in the past, we may have doubts about the nature of the solution. What are we to do, if we find that we have no other means of clearing them than the teaching of a General Council?

Another preliminary question to be settled is this: What is the nature and extent of the majority requisite in order that a decision may be considered final and infallible? May it

[1] To be sure, it is possible to conceive a Council once lawfully convoked declaring itself permanent (en permanence), and merely adjourning or proroguing its sittings from date to date. However, not even this kind of permanent Council exists at present.

be looked upon as such, if it be supported by a majority of only one, for it might have been quite different if a few whose absence was unavoidable, had been able to come to the Council? In investigating the majority, shall we take account only of numbers and not of learning also? And if so, how and by whom shall the respective authority of each voter be weighed? Evidently, it is almost as difficult, in the present state of our religious divisions, to settle this question, as to decide who should be invited to the Council. The only possible way to arrive at a solution would be to have the decision given by the almost unanimous consent of all the teachers of the world, or, at all events, of such a number of them that it could be considered unmistakably as the teaching of the whole body.

But supposing that these preliminary difficulties are overlooked or put right, can we say that we have in a General Council the speedy remedy which we said Christ must have provided against possible divisions in the faith? Certainly not.

General Councils must of necessity be rare, as teachers, especially the more important ones who would be expected to attend them, could not without great inconvenience leave their flocks for weeks and perhaps months or years, every time a question of doctrine had to be decided. In that well organised body called the Catholic Church, there were no General Councils held between 1563 and 1870, though more than one false doctrine was broached during that time and spread amongst the faithful even by heads of dioceses and local synods. No doubt a Council could meet more easily now than heretofore, owing to our improved means of communication; but telegraphs, railways and steamers are of modern introduction, and Christ had to provide a speedy solution of doubts and a prompt check to the teaching of error for the eighteen centuries that had to do without these conveniences. To ascertain the opinion of all, or of the chief teachers only, even by correspondence, would have been in the past a very slow, costly, and impracticable process. In reality, if at any period no infallible decision could be rendered except by a majority of the chief teachers in the world, we should have no means of getting rid of our doubts, of knowing the truth and of having one and the same faith. Yet, since Christ wishes to obtain this end, there must be a practical means of bringing it about.

2. **The result intended can be brought about, if that authority be vested in one man.**

As a matter of fact, reason says there is one practical way of securing these results, and that is to make one man the head of the Church with plenary and summary jurisdiction over the teachers as well as the taught, and to give him a privilege of immunity from error in matters religious, even outside such General Councils. His infallibility would enable him to give a decision which would not be liable to error, without necessarily ascertaining the opinion and weighing the authority of all, or of the chief teachers. In a Council, as well as out of it, those whose doctrine has at least his tacit approval would constitute the "infallible" teaching body (Palmieri, de Rom. Pont. 652-653). The fact that he has plenary and summary jurisdiction would enable him to enforce his decision, to deprive of all teaching authority any one—no matter how exalted his position—whose doctrine happened to be erroneous or even suspected; to forbid the faithful to listen to such a teacher, and, consequently, to accept or retain his doctrine; his supreme power would enable him to provide that none but qualified teachers should be authorised, for he could either appoint all the teachers himself, or make use of his right to cancel or ratify an appointment, or else he could appoint at least the heads by whom the others should be appointed and authorised, so that in reality no one would teach without his express or tacit approval.

Such a course could undoubtedly make unity of faith, certainty of mind, and the teaching of one and the same doctrine throughout the world *possible* at all times. All that would be wanted to make this unity of faith a *reality* would be an influence from above leading men to make a right use of their liberty and to submit to the teaching authority appointed by Christ.

Now must we conclude that Christ has undoubtedly followed this course? Our answer is that human reason cannot find out any other so likely to have been followed by Him.

No doubt, He could have granted a privilege of infallibility to every teacher; or He could have granted it to one teacher in every country, and given him plenary and summary jurisdiction over his fellow countrymen, so that from his decision there could be no appeal; or again He could have constituted or led the infallible body of teachers to establish a small oligarchy of men with plenary and summary jurisdiction over the whole world, and granted infallibility to their common decision in matters religious. Every one of these means could undoubtedly bring about and maintain unity of faith and certainty in the minds of the faithful; and none of them imply the delays of a General Council.

3. It should not be granted to a small oligarchy.

Of all the means mentioned reason declares the first we have been considering to be the best and the most likely to have been appointed by Christ. The last, being a committee like one of our Government ministries, would have to be secured against possible intestine divisions; and this possibility of disunion amongst the members of the supreme committee, not to speak of other dangers, makes it less suitable than any of the others for the end to be obtained.

4. Nor to one teacher in every country, but to one man for the whole world.

As to granting that infallibility to every teacher or to one teacher in every country, both imply the infallibility of several individual men, a privilege which supposes a miraculous intervention of the Almighty. Now God being infinite wisdom does nothing without reason, and common sense tells us that miracles must not be expected without motives; therefore since the same results, and indeed a more perfect union, can be obtained if there is one infallible head over all, we think we are right in saying that Christ must have appointed this last means in preference to the others.

VII.—**The fact that a particular teacher is at least tacitly recognised by the head of the teaching body must be the common and conclusive proof that he is authorised by Christ.**

This is but a consequence of what we have just said; if Christ gives one man full authority over the teachers and the taught, this implies that He Himself authorises no one to teach, except in due subordination to that head, and that He authorises any one who is approved by this same head.

As we said above (p. 40), He could directly point out who are the authorised teachers; but even then He could not without contradiction choose any one that would be allowed to teach independently of the head. He could also grant a teacher power to work miracles in support of his mission; but, again, He could not without contradiction grant such a privilege to any one who would not teach in due subordination to the head He has appointed. Finally, He might mean that every teacher should show that he was appointed by one who had this power of working miracles in confirmation of his mission, or at least that he was his legitimate successor; but here also, in order to be consistent, He would undoubtedly require that the teacher should have the tacit approval of the head. Therefore in Christ's intention, the common and conclusive proof that a teacher is authorised by Him, must be the fact that he is, if not appointed, at least tacitly recognised as such by the head of the teaching body. We call this fact a *conclusive* proof, since Christ cannot without inconsistency authorise any one to teach His doctrine, unless he be appointed or at least tacitly recognised as a teacher by the head. He must mean it to be the *common* and ordinary proof, since miracles are not to be expected without necessity, and since it is easy for any one to make sure that a particular teacher is at least tacitly recognised by the head of the teaching body.

We may sum up and conclude this and the previous chapter by saying that, if Christ sincerely wished men to know His doctrine, be sure of its tenets, and have one and the same faith, He must have directly or through others appointed teachers, authorised by Himself or in His name to impart it to the world; He must moreover have made them infallible as a body; He must have placed over them, as their head, one man endowed with infallibility in matters religious whenever he intends giving an infallible decision, and lastly must have granted that man plenary and summary jurisdiction over the teachers and the taught, so that his express or tacit approval given to a man is the conclusive proof that he is authorised by our Lord Himself to teach His doctrine.

CHAPTER V.

HISTORY TEACHES THAT CHRIST APPOINTED THE VERY MEANS OF ENABLING MEN TO KNOW HIS DOCTRINE, WHICH COMMON SENSE DECLARES HE MUST HAVE CHOSEN.

WE have shown in the last chapter that, if Christ wished all men to know His doctrine and consequently be sure of its tenets and have one and the same faith, He must have appointed an infallible teaching authority under one infallible head. In the present chapter we purpose to confirm the finding of common sense by proving from historical documents that He did appoint that very means to obtain the end He had in view. Our chief authority will be the Bible; but lest we should be accused of interpreting it to suit our own fancies, we shall produce other authorities as well. These will show the belief of men who lived nearer to the time of Christ than we do, and had more facility than we have of knowing from the Apostles what He did, said, and meant. Their belief was precisely what we find expressed in the Bible, viz., that Christ gave a certain number of men an exclusive right to teach His doctrine, endowed them with infallibility in matters religious, placed over them a man with plenary jurisdiction also endowed with the same infallibility, and intended that body of teachers to be till the end of time the means of propagating His doctrine and bringing about and maintaining unity of faith.

Art. I.—Christ has appointed an infallible teaching authority, which He intends to exist till the end of time.

I.—**Christ has given a body of men authority to teach His doctrine, and even to rule and govern the faithful.**

Our Lord chose and appointed a body of men, whom He sent to teach what He Himself had taught or what the Holy

Ghost would reveal to them; He even did more, for if we wish to express the extent of the authority He granted them, we must add that He also gave them power to rule and govern the faithful, to forgive and retain sins, and made them ministers and dispensers of the mysteries of God. We find all this clearly stated in the New Testament.

1. The evangelists Matthew and Mark tell us that Jesus singled out twelve of His disciples, and that to eleven of them (after the death of Judas) He gave *authority to teach:* "Go ye, teach all nations .... He that believeth not shall be condemned;"[1] "You are the light of the world" (Matt. v. 14); "He that heareth you heareth Me; he that despiseth you despiseth Me" (Luke x. 16).

They were not to teach everything they might choose, but only what God had revealed, *what Christ had taught, and what the Holy Ghost would teach them;* they were consequently to speak as witnesses of what they had seen and heard: "He opened their understanding that they might understand the Scriptures" (Luke xxiv. 45); "Go ye, preach the Gospel. ... teach ye all nations ... to observe all things whatsoever I have commanded you" (Mark xvi. 15, 16; Matt. xxviii. 19, 20); "I will ask the Father, and He shall give you another Paraclete. ... He will teach you all things and bring all things to your mind whatsoever I shall have said to you" (John xiv. 16, 26); "You shall receive the power of the Holy Ghost ... and you shall be witnesses unto Me in Jerusalem and in all Judæa and Samaria, and even to the uttermost part of the earth" (Acts i. 8).

He gave them *authority to rule and govern* the faithful by granting them power to place men under certain *obligations:* "Whatsoever you shall bind upon earth shall be bound also in heaven" (Matt. xviii. 18). He even gave them power to *judge* of the most secret thoughts and actions and *forgive sins:* "Receive ye the Holy Ghost, whose sins you shall forgive they are forgiven them, and whose sins you shall retain they are retained" (John xx. 22, 23). He gave them the *right to punish,* in order to protect effectually faith and morals: they are allowed to deprive the culprit of certain spiritual advantages, and even to exclude him from the society of the faithful: "If [thy brother] will not hear them

---

Matt. xxviii. 19, 20; Mark xvi. 15, 16.

[the two or three witnesses], tell the Church; and if he will not hear the Church, let him be to thee as the heathen and publican. Amen I say to you, whatsoever you shall bind upon earth, shall be bound also in heaven, and whatsoever you shall loose upon earth, shall be loosed also in heaven" (Matt. xviii. 17, 18).

As His Father had sent Him, He also sent them and constituted them His *ministers* and the *dispensers* of the mysteries of God, *i.e.*, of His doctrine and of His sacraments.[1]

But lest the gift of this great authority might lead to pride of heart, He warned them not to imitate the Pharisees, not to allow others to call them masters, and not to behave as "the princes of the gentiles who lord it over them" (Matt. xx. 25), but to remain meek and humble like Himself (Matt. xx. 28).

2. Did the *Apostles understand* that they were authorised to teach and even to rule and govern the faithful? Yes, for we see them make use of that authority. They teach men by word of mouth or by writing; and in teaching they refer to what they know through revelation (Gal. i. 11, 12), or to what is found in the Scriptures (Acts i. 16; ii. 16; xiii. 22, 33-35), or again to what they have seen or heard (1 John i. 1-3). They remind the faithful that they have received their *mission from God*, not from men: "Paul, an apostle not of men, neither by man, but by Jesus Christ and God the Father" (Gal. i. 1). "God indeed hath set some in the Church, first Apostles, secondly prophets, thirdly doctors. . . . Are all Apostles? are all prophets? are all doctors?" (1 Cor. xii. 28-29).

Elsewhere we see them make laws, punish sinners, impose penalties (Acts xv. 28; 1 Cor. v. 4-5; 2 Cor. x. 6.) "What will you?" says St. Paul to the Corinthians, "Shall I come to you with a rod?" (1 Cor. iv. 21). They invite the faithful to express their opinion about the men to be elected (Acts vi. 3), but they themselves decide and *give authority* to teach and govern: "I have left thee in Crete, that thou shouldest set in order the things that are wanting and shouldest ordain priests in every city, as I also appointed thee" (Tit. i. 5).

---

[1] Matt xxviii. 19; Luke xxii. 19; John xx. 23; Cf. 1 Cor. i. 13-17; iv. 1.

They tell those they appoint: "The Holy Ghost hath placed you to rule the Church of God .... take heed to yourselves and to the whole flock" (Acts xx 28).

Therefore both from what the Apostles did and said, and from the words of our Divine Lord, we may conclude that, as a means to spread His doctrine throughout all nations and bring about unity of faith amongst men, Christ chose and appointed teachers to whom He gave authority not only to propound His doctrine but even to rule and govern the faithful, and that the appointment and the authority of these pastors came, not from men, but directly from Christ Himself.

II.—**The teachers chosen and appointed by Christ were granted a privilege of immunity from error in matters of faith and morals, if not individually, at least as a body.**

1. This privilege is clearly implied in the following words of our Lord as related in the Gospel: "All power is given Me in heaven and in earth: going therefore teach ye all nations, baptizing them in the name of the Father and of the Son and of the Holy Ghost; teaching them to observe all things whatsoever I have commanded you: and behold I am with you all days even to the consummation of the world" (Matt. xxviii. 18-20); "I will ask the Father, and He shall give you another Paraclete, that He may abide with you for ever. . . . He will teach you all things and bring all things to your mind, whatsoever I shall have said to you" (John xiv. 16, 26); "He that heareth you, heareth Me; and he that despiseth you, despiseth Me" (Luke x. 16); "He that believeth not shall be condemned" (Mark xvi. 16); "If he will not hear the Church, let him be to thee as the heathen and publican" (Matt. xviii. 17); "Upon this rock I will build my Church, and the gates of hell shall not prevail against it" (Matt. xvi. 18).

From these texts it is clear that the Apostles, if not as individuals (for Christ does not address them individually), at least considered as a body, cannot fall into error, that is, are infallible in expounding the doctrines which He commissioned them to teach; as it is manifest that neither Christ nor the Holy Ghost could truly be said to be with them, whilst teaching falsehood. Consequently if they were liable to error, our Lord could not promise to be *always* with them, or declare that the Holy Ghost would always be with them, or assert that he *who hears them hears Him!* Still less could He say that " He who does not believe *shall be condemned*," as it would be unjust to condemn a man who, knowing that his teachers are fallible and hearing them speak of things beyond the reach of human reason (as mysteries are), questions if they be not mistaken, and for a time suspends his judgment or even refuses to believe what seems to him untrue; such a man should rather be praised than condemned! Lastly Christ could not say that the *gates of hell* shall not prevail against the Church ; for if her teachers as a body could ever lead her into error, falsehood, which is one of the powers of hell, would truly prevail. [1]

2. Should these texts seem obscure and mysterious, we have in the writings and doings of the *Apostles* a clear interpretation of them. St. Paul speaks of himself and of the Apostles as being " *Ambassadors, God as it were exhorting by us* " (2 Cor. v. 20). Therefore, in his eyes, these ambassadors, at least taken as a body, cannot teach error, as otherwise God could not be said to speak by them. "Though we or an angel from heaven," he says elsewhere, "preach a gospel to you besides that which we have preached to you, *let him be anathema*" (Gal. i. 8). He could not claim in clearer terms to be infallible. He writes that Christ desires unity of faith in His Church and also that firm conviction in the minds of the faithful which will enable them to resist sophisms ; and he adds that, *in order to* obtain this twofold end, "He gave some apostles .... and other some pastors and doctors" (Ephes. iv. 11-14). It is evident, St. Paul intends to convey that these men are safeguarded from erring in doctrine: otherwise the faithful could not feel sure that they were taught the truth, and ceasing to trust those teachers, might listen to others, *be tossed*

---

[1] The expression " The gates of hell " means " hell " itself, those who have power in hell, Satan and his angels. Cf. Deuteronomy xxi. 19 ; xxii. 15 ; xxv. 7 ; Ruth iv. 1 et seq. ; Job. v. 4 ; xxxi. 21 ; Prov. xxii. 22 ; Isaias xxix. 21 ; Amos v. 10, 15 ; Esther iii. 2, 3 ; iv. 2, 6 ; v. 9, 13 ; vi. 12 ; Daniel ii. 49. "The Porte" means the Royal Palace, the "head" of Turkey, even in our days. See Patrizzi, de. interp. Script. Sacr. L. 2, 9, 10. Art. iii. sec, 1, Arg. 2. Palmieri, De Rom. Pont. p. 330.

to and fro and carried about with every wind of doctrine, and end by holding different views.

Elsewhere the same Apostle calls *the Church "the pillar and ground of the truth"* (1 Tim. iii. 15); and as her teachers have everything to do with her knowledge of the truth, we may again infer that, in his judgment, they cannot, as a body, propound false doctrines: for this liability, and as a consequence the possibility that the Church can err, would be against the truth rather than in favour of it.

In confirmation of this the Apostles speak of *their own view* on a point of faith as being *the view of the Holy Ghost* Himself, a fact alone sufficient to warrant us in believing that they considered themselves infallible. We are here alluding to the first Council of Jerusalem, when the Apostles met in order to decide whether a man might be saved without following the Mosaic observances: "It hath seemed good to the Holy Ghost and to us to lay no farther burden upon you," was the sentence promulgated by the Apostles (Acts xv. 28), their words clearly implying that in settling that question of faith (Acts xv. 1) they deemed themselves infallible and wished others to regard them as such.

3. As a matter of fact, probably most of our readers believe that they were infallible, nay inspired, even *as individuals*,—at least while writing the sacred books of the New Testament,—for some of the texts we have quoted seem to point out that they were infallible as individuals not only in writing, but in teaching by word of mouth.[1] But whether the teachers chosen and appointed by Christ were infallible as individuals or not, we think we have sufficiently proved that they were, *at least as a body*, not only authorised by our Lord to teach, rule and govern, in His Church, but also endowed by Him with infallibility in teaching His doctrine.

However, a more important point to consider is whether it was the will of Christ that these first teachers should be succeeded by others possessed of the same rights and privileges.

We said in the last chapter that He must have intended that men should until the end of time be taught by authorised masters endowed with infallibility; we now proceed to show

---

[1] They show also that St. Paul, though he became a member of that teaching body only after the death of Christ, had the same rights and privileges as the first chosen Apostles.

from the same historical sources that He did mean His Apostles to have successors to the end of time, if not with all their rights and privileges, at least with an exclusive right to teach His doctrine, to rule and govern the faithful, and with a privilege of infallibility as a body, whenever they taught what He commissioned them to teach.

III.—Christ meant that His Apostles should have till the end of time successors authorised both to teach His doctrine and to govern the faithful.

1. His words already quoted make this sufficiently clear to allow us to be brief. "Going, teach ye *all nations* . . . . I am with you all days even to the *consummation of the world*" (Matt. xxviii. 19, 20). As Christ knows that those men He is sending will die long before "all nations" are taught, and long before the end of time, it is evident that He means them to have others associated with them to help, and even to succeed them.

"The gates of hell *shall not prevail* against" the Church, says Christ. These words also imply that the teaching body will never die or cease to teach His doctrine; for if, through the death of the teachers, the doctrine of Christ could ever cease to be propagated, the powers of hell—death and ignorance—would prevail, and our Lord's promise would be a vain word.

Do these texts prove that the Apostles are to have successors not only as teachers, but also as *rulers*, in the Church? Yes; for those whom Christ was addressing were a body of rulers as well as of teachers, and we have just said that that body is to last for ever.

2. But we are the more certain about our conclusion, as the *Apostles* themselves, who had every opportunity of knowing the mind of Christ on this matter, make it quite evident, by what they said, wrote and did, that our Lord intended that they should have successors both as teachers and rulers.

In several places of the New Testament, we find the words "bishops, priests or presbyters;" [1] in 1 Tim. v. 19, we

[1] Phil. i. 1; Titus i. 5; 1 Tim. v. 19, 22; Acts xx. 17, 28; I Peter v. 1.

are distinctly told that a bishop is superior to a priest, though the same word is often applied to bishops and priests. But whatever their name may be, it is clear there are in the Church *men appointed* by the Apostles *to teach Christ's doctrine*, for St. Paul says that "a bishop must be without crime .... that he may be able to exhort in sound doctrine and to convince the gainsayers" (Titus i. 7, 9); " These things speak," he writes to Titus (Titus ii. 15); and to Timothy, " Preach the Word" (2 Tim. iv. 2 ; Cf. 1 Tim. vi., 20 ; 2 Tim. ii. 2).

These men have also authority *to rule and govern the faithful*, for St. Paul says to Timothy : " Be instant in season, out of season ; reprove, entreat, rebuke in all patience and doctrine, do the work of an evangelist, fulfil thy ministry" (2 Tim. iv. 2, 5); and to Titus : " Exhort and rebuke with all authority. Let no man despise thee" (Titus ii. 15); and to the clergy of Ephesus : "Take heed to yourselves and to the whole flock, wherein the Holy Ghost has placed you bishops to rule the Church of God" (Acts xx. 28). "The ancients that are amongst you I beseech, who am myself also an ancient and a witness of the sufferings of Christ .... feed the flock of God which is amongst you" writes St. Peter, . . . " Ye young men be subject to the ancients " (1 Peter v. 1, 2, 5 ; Cf. 1 Tim. v. 1, 7.)

The book of the Acts tells us that *the ancients*, as well as the Apostles themselves, *made laws* for the faithful: Paul "went through Syria and Cilicia, confirming the churches, commanding them to keep the precepts of the apostles *and* the ancients " (Acts xv. 41). "Obey your prelates and be subject to them," writes St. Paul to the Hebrews, "for they watch, as being to render an account of your souls" (Heb. xiii. 17). He does not deny to Timothy the right to judge even priests, though he warns him not to receive accusations too readily : " Against a priest receive not an accusation but under two or three witnesses " (1 Tim. v. 19).

These teachers and rulers form *one moral body* with the apostles, being appointed by, and receiving their authority[1] from them : a clear proof that they are intended to help them, and to strengthen, renew and perpetuate the one teaching body appointed by our Lord, and so obviate the possibility of witnessing the spectacle of two or more independent and

---

[1] With one exception, see below, p. 104.

opposing sets of teachers, a state of things different from what our Lord established. "For this cause *I* left thee in Crete, that thou shouldest set in order the things that are wanting, and shouldest ordain priests in every city, as I also appointed thee" (Titus i. 5); "The things which thou hast heard of me by many witnesses, the same commend to faithful men who shall be fit to teach others also" (2 Tim. ii. 2; cf. Acts xiv. 22 ; xv. 24). This moral body must exist "until," as St. Paul says, "we all meet into the unity of faith and of the knowledge of the Son of God, unto a perfect man, unto the measure of the age of the fulness of Christ," that is to say until the end of the world (Eph. iv. 13). For "how shall they hear without a preacher? How shall they preach, unless they be *sent?*" (Rom. x. 14, 15.)

"Impose not hands lightly upon any man," says St. Paul to Timothy (1 Tim. v. 22). These last words allude not only to a bishop's power, but to the *religious rite* by which a man was admitted into the body of teachers in the Church, and which consisted of an imposition of hands. The same apostle alludes to it again, when he writes to Timothy: "Stir up the grace of God which is in thee by the imposition of my hands" (2 Tim. i. 6); "Neglect not the grace that is in thee, which was given thee by prophecy with imposition of the hands of the priesthood" (1 Tim iv. 14). This is the rite known by the name of "ordination," [1] which, together with the "mission" received to teach and rule, constitutes that *apostolic succession*, looked upon by the early Christians as the test whereby all cities that claimed to belong to the true Church could be known to belong to it or not.

3. From what we have said it is natural to conclude that this right to teach and rule must have been claimed and used by the *bishops of the early centuries*, and recognised in them by the faithful.

As a matter of fact, history discovers to us bishops instructing and governing the faithful throughout the world, appointing men to help them in their work and to preside as teachers and rulers over the various districts. They meet now and then to solve doubts and difficulties, to decide controversies, to censure new doctrines and to excommunicate both heretics and those who might refuse to submit to

---

[1] Titus i. 5; Acts xiv. 22 ; cf. Canon. Apost. in Constit. Apost. 1. 8, c. 4 and seq. ; Canon. Syn. Carth. 2, 3, anno 398.

their decisions : they condemn the Judaising party at the Council of Jerusalem, Paul of Samosata at Antioch (A.D. 268), Arius at Nicea (A.D. 325), Macedonius at Constantinople (A D. 381), Eutyches at Chalcedon (A.D. 451), Nestorius at Ephesus (A.D. 481), etc.; and when their decision was sanctioned by the Bishop of Rome, it put an end to the controversy, although, as may be easily understood, it did not always convince those who were condemned.

4. In reality, the right to instruct the faithful in religious matters is implicitly recognised by all those who believe in the *ministry*, even when the authority to govern is for them a matter of doubt. A Christian admitting the ministry of teachers implicitly confesses that, in the Church of Christ, some have authority over others, if not to govern, at least to teach them. He may happen to think that their authority comes from the community that appoints them; but even then, one thing seems certain, he believes that the existence of teachers till the end of time is in accordance with the intentions of Christ. We have shown how correct this view is; we have proved also that Christ meant some at least of those teachers to be rulers in His Church. We may therefore conclude that it is an historical fact that Christ gave a body of men a right to teach His doctrine and govern the faithful until the end of time.

But we said (p. 52) that the men appointed by our Lord were infallible at least as a body; and we may wonder whether such a body, when composed of entirely new members, still preserved and is meant to preserve till the end of time, that privilege of infallibility. The following is the answer furnished by history.

IV.—Christ meant the teachers to be infallible as a body till the end of time.

1. That Christ intended the teachers to be infallible to the end of the world is clearly shown from the fact that He granted the privilege of infallibility to His Apostles taken as a body (p. 52), and that He meant them, as such, to exist till the end of time (p. 55). If a society obtains a privilege, it is not supposed to lose it from the fact that new members join it, unless, of course, there should be in the granting of the privilege a clear statement to that effect. Now there is no such restriction

in the words of our Lord, nor in those of St. Paul which we have quoted (p. 52 and seq.); on the contrary, some of them show most explicitly that the teaching body will *never* cease to be infallible: "Teach ye all nations. . . . I am with you all days even *to the consummation of the world*" (Matt. xxviii. 19, 20); "The Paraclete . . . . will abide with you *for ever*" (John xiv. 16); "The gates of hell *shall not prevail*" against the Church (Matt. xvi. 18); God has given some Apostles, and other some pastors and doctors . . . . in order that "*henceforth* we be no more children tossed to and fro and carried about with every wind of doctrine" (Eph. iv. 11-14). The Church "*is* . . . . the pillar and ground of the truth" (1. Tim. iii. 15). Such expressions and promises clearly imply that the teachers, as a body, will be infallible to the end of time.

2. We said above (p. 40) that if the end Christ had in view was to be attained, the privilege of infallibility was *indispensable* to the teachers taken as a body. If so, it is evident that Christ did not mean that privilege, granted by Him to the Apostles, to cease after their death, when it became less easy to preserve unity of faith.

3. At all events, the *primitive Church* did not think it had ceased after the death of the Apostles; for whenever a point of doctrine was defined by a General Council and the decision confirmed by the Bishop of Rome, it was looked upon as irrevocably settled; and whenever an heretical doctrine was condemned and its condemnation sanctioned by the Bishop of Rome, it was looked upon as condemned in the same degree. History proves that matters of doctrine were settled at each of the first General Councils, and looked upon as definitely concluded when the Bishop of Rome had sanctioned their decision (see p. 84 and seq). It is evident this could not have been the case if the teachers with the Bishop of Rome, considered as one body, had not been regarded as infallible in matters of belief.

3. To such of our readers as believe in "the *holy* Catholic *Church*" all we have written about the infallibility of her teachers must seem superfluous. Any man who believes that the Church of Christ is holy, implicitly admits that her teachers, taken as a body, are infallible in their teaching; for it is evident that the Church could not be said to be holy, if she did not contain in herself the foundation of holiness, viz., a wholesome doctrine, free from error and leading men to sound

morality. But the doctrine depends upon the teachers; it is therefore obvious that any one who believes that the Church's doctrine is and must be free from error, implicitly believes that her teachers as a body must teach the truth and cannot teach falsehood. We trust that even such as do not believe in the holiness of Christ's Church have found in the proofs we have given sufficient reasons to draw the same conclusion.

Art. II. Christ has placed the teachers and the taught under one head, endowed with full authority and infallibility, whom He intends to exist till the end of time.

We added that Christ placed the teachers and the taught under one infallible head, so that when, in the previous pages, we spoke of the teaching body, we always included the head, without which a body cannot be complete. We have therefore to prove from historical documents that Christ appointed a head over the teachers and rulers, endowed him with infallibility in matters of faith and morals, and meant him to have successors with the same prerogatives and privileges till the end of time.

I.—Christ appointed a head over the Apostles in the person of Peter.

1. If we consult the New Testament, we find our Lord (*a*) as it were *preparing* Peter for that supremacy over the whole Church.

He promised to change his name of "Simon" into "Cephas," Petra, Petrus, Rock (John i. 42). Now God never changed or gave a name in the Scriptures, except when something extraordinary had been or was about to be done. (See why Abram was called Abraham, in Gen. xvii. 5; Sarai, Sara, in Gen. xvii. 15; Jacob, Israel, in Gen. xxxii. 28; Elizabeth's and Zachariah's son, John, in Luke i. 13; the Messias, Jesus, in Matt. i. 21).

He placed Peter above the other disciples on several occasions: for example, He paid the tribute for Himself and Peter, not for the others (Matt. xvii. 26); He went up into Simon's boat (Luke v. 3); after the miraculous draught of fishes, when Peter, James, John, and the others were all astonished, He spoke to Peter alone, and said to him: " Henceforth thou shalt catch men " (Luke v. 10); He prayed for him in particular, and told him to confirm his brethren (Luke xxii. 32); Peter was the first Apostle whose feet He washed (John xiii. 6), and to whom He appeared after His resurrection (Luke xxiv. 34); he alone was mentioned when the angel ordered the holy women to tell the disciples that Christ would be before them in Galilee (Mark xvi. 7); he alone was enabled to walk on the sea (Matt. xiv. 28, 29). Surely a mere coincidence could not account for this preference so often shown to Peter; there must be some reason for it, and we have a well-founded one, if, as we hold, Christ was preparing him for the supremacy.

(*b*) More than once He expressed His intention, and *promised* to make him the foundation of His Church and to give him the keys of His kingdom.—" Thou art Peter, and upon this rock I will build my Church " (Matt. xvi. 18), or in Syriac or the Chaldaic used by Christ, " Thou art Kepha, and upon this Kepha . . . . ," in Latin, " Tu es Petra, et super hanc Petram . . . . thou art the rock and upon this rock . . . . " By these words our Lord actually changes Simon's name into that of " rock," which has become " Peter," and promises that Peter shall have in the Church the same function and importance which the foundation has in a building. Now the foundation gives the building its unity, strength and firmness, and the whole edifice rests upon it; therefore Peter will perform the same office in the Church and give to it unity, strength and firmness. But the Church is a body of men; and in such only a ruling authority can maintain these essentials. Therefore, we must conclude, Christ promised this ruling authority over the Church to Peter.

Our Lord adds: " I will give to thee the keys of the kingdom of heaven " (Matt. xvi. 19). Now, to hand anybody the keys of a house or town is to give him full authority over the house or town. [1] We must therefore admit that Christ here promises to grant Peter full authority over the kingdom of heaven, that is to say over His Church, for His Church alone can be that kingdom of heaven, since of it He says elsewhere that it contains not only wise but foolish virgins. [2]

Christ continues : " Whatsoever thou shalt bind upon earth, it shall be bound also in heaven; and whatsoever thou shalt loose on earth it shall be loosed also in heaven " (Matt. xvi.

---

[1] Cf. Isaias xxii. 22 ; Apoc. iii. 7 ; i. 18.
[2] Cf. Matt iv. 17 ; Mark i. 15 ; Matt. v. 3 ; xiii. 11 ; Luke vi. 20; viii. 10, etc. ; John xviii. 36 ; Apoc. xxi. 2.

19). In these words our Lord promises an unlimited power to Peter, the jurisdiction of a king over His Church, over the faithful as well as over the Apostles. There cannot be any doubt that the Saviour here promises to give him authority even over the Apostles, for His words are an answer to Peter's profession of faith, and express the "reward" he will receive for it in return: "Blessed art thou, Simon bar-jona: because flesh and blood hath not revealed it to thee, but my Father who is in heaven; and I say to thee that thou are Peter, and upon this rock I will build My Church . . . . and I will give to thee the keys of the kingdom of heaven, and whatsoever thou shalt bind upon earth, it shall be bound also in heaven, and whatsoever thou shalt loose on earth, it shall be loosed also in heaven" (Matt. xvi. 17-19). Later on, our Lord says to all the Apostles: "Whatever you shall bind upon earth, shall be bound also in heaven; and whatever you shall loose upon earth, shall be loosed also in heaven" (Matt. xviii. 18). But in this authority bestowed upon the Apostles, there is and must be a restriction: for if they receive the same power as was promised to St. Peter, the latter has obtained no reward for his public profession of faith, though Christ had singled him out of the twelve to promise him a special recompense. Our Lord, on that occasion, promised to him alone, and not to the others, a full and complete jurisdiction over all and for all cases: therefore Peter can "bind" the Apostles; they cannot bind him, any more than they could bind each other. Peter possesses all the authority they possess; they have not all the power that he has; they can bind only the faithful, whereas he can lay obligations on the faithful and the Apostles as well; he can free the faithful from the laws made by the latter, while they cannot free any one from obligations imposed by him. Peter alone is the rock, he alone has the keys.

Three texts of Scripture seem to be in contradiction to what we say. In the first, St. Paul calls all the Apostles, and not Peter alone, the foundation upon which we are built: "You are built upon the foundation of the Apostles and prophets, Jesus Christ Himself being the chief corner stone" (Eph. ii. 20). Therefore, it is objected, St. Paul denies that Peter is the only foundation, and consequently that he is the head of the Church. To this we answer that, just as these words do not show that the prophets are equal to the Apostles, though like them the foundation upon which we are built, in the same way they do not prove that, considered as the foundation of the Church, the Apostles are all equal, and that Peter is not their superior.

In the second text St. Paul says that Christ is the rock: "All drank the same spiritual drink, and they drank of the spiritual rock that followed them, and the rock was Christ" (1 Cor x. 4); and the objection is that, as there cannot be two foundations, Peter is not the one. Our answer is that, in this passage the rock is not alluded to as the "foundation" of the Church, but as the "source of all graces."

However, in the third text St. Paul clearly says that our Saviour is the foundation and that there is no other foundation but Him: "Other foundation no man lay but that which is laid: which is Christ Jesus" (1 Cor. iii. 11). But here also, if we refer to the context, we see that Christ is not spoken of as the *rock* on which the Church is built and by which her unity is preserved,[1] but as the *object of* St. Paul's *teaching:* what the Apostle taught concerning Him is the basis on which the sanctification of the Ephesians must rest; his successors must not lay a different foundation but simply continue what he has begun.

(c) Christ made good His promise and *appointed* Peter the head of the Church, for He gave him the supreme power to teach and rule.

Doubtless He must have given him that supreme jurisdiction over all, since He promised it and added no condition to His promise; so that, even if the Evangelists did not tell us when Jesus fulfilled it, we may feel sure that, at some time or other, He did so. However in St. John (John xxi. 15 and seq.) we find an account of its fulfilment by our Lord.

Christ had already given Peter and the Apostles their mission and apostolic authority (John xx. 21); now He gives something more to Peter as a reward of his love: He says to him, "Feed My lambs . . . feed My sheep," and thus makes him a shepherd. A shepherd's office is to give his sheep their food, to lead, watch over, and defend them; and such is

---

[1] Of course, Christ, and not Peter, is the *primary foundation* of the Church. Peter, the rock on which she is built, rests on that primary foundation.

also the proper meaning of the Greek word βόσχε or ποίμαινε, which is here translated by "feed." It applies to men watching over sheep; it is also applicable to kings, who are called by Homer "the pastors of nations, ποιμένας λαῶν," as Cyrus is called "shepherd" by God (Isaias xliv. 28).[1]

Therefore Peter's office is to provide with food, to lead, watch over, and defend the lambs and sheep entrusted to his care. The lambs and sheep mean the whole "fold," the Church of Christ; we must consequently infer that our Lord, by the words "Feed My lambs .... feed My sheep," gives Peter authority to lead, to watch over, to rule and govern the teachers as well as the taught, *i.e.*, His whole Church. The food of the members of the Church is religious truth, Christ's doctrine, and the various means of sanctification: we cannot therefore fail to arrive at the conclusion that our Lord gives him authority to teach His doctrine, dispense the mysteries of God, and do all that can be done to preserve the lambs and sheep from error and sin; we must also conclude that both the lambs and the sheep, i.e. the whole flock, are bound to submit to his direction and accept his teaching and ruling, since he is their divinely appointed superior in all religious matters. Whether Christ invited him to show his love for his master, by acting as pastor of His Church, or meant to tell him how much he should love One who was making him the head of His fold, or again wished to reward him for his love, which is more likely — it is clear that by making him pastor of His Church He did make him the supreme head of the Apostles and the faithful, of whom His fold was composed.

In Luke (xxii. 31, 32) Christ says to Peter: "Simon, Simon, behold Satan hath desired to have you that he may sift you as wheat; but I have prayed for thee that thy faith fail not; and thou, being once converted, confirm thy brethren." If Peter is to confirm his brethren in the faith, we can entertain no doubt but that he is duly qualified to discharge this duty, and consequently has authority to show them what is true and what is not, and also to guide and govern them, that they may the better avoid error and do what is required in order to keep their faith.

---

[1] Cf 2 Kings v. 2, vii. 7; Ezech. xxxvii. 24; Psalms xxii. 1; Matt. ii. 6.

2. Judging from facts, Peter, the Apostles and the faithful act and speak as if he were truly the head of the Church. We do not say that what the Apostles do or write necessarily implies that they looked upon Peter as one who had jurisdiction over them, but we hold that they could not have acted or spoken differently, if Peter had truly possessed that jurisdiction; and knowing, as we do, what our Lord said of and to Peter, we naturally conclude that the Apostles acted and spoke as they did, because they were convinced of the supreme authority of Peter over the whole Church.

Peter stands and speaks first, when there is question of completing the Apostolic College; after receiving the Holy Ghost, he stands up with the eleven, but he alone speaks to the Jews; he alone judges, condemns and punishes Ananias and Saphira, and Simon the Magician; in the Council of Jerusalem he proposes what is to be done on the question of circumcision and is the first to give his opinion; he visits the churches of Galilee, Judæa and Samaria as a general reviews his troops, says St. Chrysostom;[1] the faithful ask him what they are to do and, though they also apply to the other Apostles, Peter alone answers them; he alone has a vision about the reception of the gentiles and stops the murmurs of the Jews; his miracles, not those of the other Apostles, are recorded at length.[2] Peter was chosen by the Apostles to go to Samaria with St. John, or, to use the sacred writer's words, "he was sent," just as Paul and Barnabas were sent by the faithful of Antioch to consult the Apostles—that is to say, he was asked to go; of this we see no other reason except that, being the head of the Apostles, he was the better able to preserve the Samaritans from the influence of Simon the Magician. Sixteen times is his name mentioned in the first place, or alone, in the Scriptures, though the other Apostles are with him. There are only four cases in which his name is not given first: in 1 Cor. i. 12, iii. 22, ix. 5, it is mentioned last, but in these texts the most honourable place is the last; in Gal. ii. 9 James is mentioned before him, but Bellarmine observes that Peter's name was cited first in the copies used by SS. Ambrose, Chrysostom, Augustine, Jerome and by Theodoret. At all events there would be a reason not to mention his name first, if St. Paul meant to give the order in which he was received by the Apostles in

---

[1] Homil. xxi. in Act.   [2] Cf. Acts i. 15; ii. 14; v. ; viii; xv. 7; viii. 25; ix. 32; ii. 37, 38; x. ; xi. ; v. ; vii. ; ix. ; xii; viii. 14.

Jerusalem (he saw James first, and so mentions him first), or if he wished specially to honour the bishop of Jerusalem, St. James: however, one thing is certain, not knowing what was his motive, we cannot infer that he did not consider Peter as superior to James (Cf. Palmieri, ibid., 373). On the contrary, we have reason to believe the opposite, for he tells us that he went to Jerusalem on purpose to see Peter, and, though James was the bishop of the city, he does not say that he went to see anyone else (Gal. i. 18).

If Peter is, as we hold, the head of the Apostolic College, we may feel sure that history will relate nothing tending to prove that in the fulfilment of their mission the Apostles did not always act in due subordination to him. Of course it does not follow that they might not defend their own views and respectfully show that he should adopt the same himself, if opportunity required or allowed such a course. While ready to obey, subjects are often justified in enlightening their superiors. Indeed St. Paul does not hide that he used this right (Gal. ii. 11): Peter, though convinced that the Mosaic law was no longer binding (Acts xv. 7, 28, 29), was following it on one particular point, that the Jews might not be scandalized; this was an imprudent concession, nothing more, but St. Paul objected to it. However the fact that he said nothing to James and Barnabas shows that, in his opinion, these would naturally follow Peter, if the latter could be made to give up his practice; consequently, if maturely considered, St. Paul's action proves that he looked upon Peter as the head of the Church.

One single passage might be put forward as apparently showing that the Apostles did not regard Peter as their superior; and that is where St. Luke says that "there was a strife amongst them which of them should seem to be greater" (Luke xxii. 24). But this merely proves that, before the resurrection, they did not think Peter had as yet any authority over them, or that, not having received the Holy Ghost, they perhaps did not clearly understand that he was to be their superior. Yet the fact of their asking such a question indicates that they had some doubts about it. At all events, Jesus does not deny in His answer that one was to be greater than the others; on the contrary, He clearly admits it, for He tells them how he who is the greater amongst them, should behave: "He that is the greater amongst you, let him become as

the younger ; and he that is the leader, as he that serveth. . .
I am in the midst of you as he that serveth " (Luke xxii. 26,
27). Why make a rule for the superior and leader, if there is
to be no superior or leader amongst them ?

3. As we have already observed (p. 65), the way in which
the sacred writers and the Apostles speak of Peter, and
likewise the manner in which he himself speaks and acts,
as related in the New Testament, may not necessarily
imply that he had, in their eyes, authority over the whole
Church, themselves included. But those who lived nearer
to the Apostles did unmistakably consider him as the head of
the Apostolic College and of the Church. To our mind this
clearly demonstrates that the Apostles themselves regarded
him as their chief and spoke of him as such to the faithful ;
for, as we shall show below, there is no other possible
explanation for the conviction which so universally prevailed
amongst the *early Christians.*

To prove this general belief : Origen[1] (who died 254) writes :
" See what Christ says to Peter, the great foundation-stone of
the Church, the strongest rock on which Christ founded
His Church : O thou of little faith, why didst thou doubt?"
St. Optatus of Milevis[2] (+ 375) addressing Parmenian, says :
" You cannot affect ignorance of the fact that the episcopal
chair was first established by Peter, the head of all the
Apostles." That " blessed Peter, placed above all the
disciples, is the one to whom the keys of the kingdom of
heaven are entrusted " says St. Basil[3] (+ 379) ; St. Cyril of
Jerusalem[4] (+ 386), and St. Gregory Nazianzen[5] (+ 390) call
him "the prince of the Apostles." St. Epiphanius[6] (+ 403) says:
" He chose Peter to be the leader of the disciples," and[7]
speaks of him as being " the first of the Apostles, the one to
whom the flock is entrusted." St. Chrysostom[8] (+ 407) calls
him " the pastor and head of the Church." " Among the
twelve," writes St. Jerome (+ 420), " one is chosen out, that, by

---

[1] Origen, Homil. 5. in Exod. no. 4. Migne.
[2] De Schism. Don. lib. ii., n. 2, Galland.
[3] In Proœm. de Judic Dei No. 7 and adv. Eunom. lib. 2, no. 4. Migne.
[4] In Cat. ii. xi. xvii. Migne.
[5] In Carmen de seipso and adv. Episc.
[6] Adv. Hær. Alog. 51. Petavius.
[7] In Ancor. n. 9. Petavius.
[8] Hom. de 10,000 talentis ; hom. 32 in Matt. ; hom. 3 in Act. ; hom. 72 in Joan. Migne.

the appointment of a head, the opportunity for schism might be taken away."[1] "Peter alone in the whole world is chosen," says St. Leo the Great, "to superintend the conversion of all nations and to have authority over all the Apostles and all the fathers of the Church, so that, although there are, in the people of God, many priests and many pastors, Peter truly rules them all whom Christ rules above him."[2]

4. We might add that, because they looked upon the Bishop of Rome as Peter's successor in that see, the early Christians considered him as the head of the Church (p. 73): see below, quotations from St. Cyril (p. 73), Pope Gelasius, Council of Arles (p. 77), St. Cyprian (p. 82), Optatus (p. 73), Peter Chrysologus (p. 74) : this of course implies the belief that Peter himself was the head of the Church. But what we have said seems to us sufficient to establish our proposition, and we think we may look upon it as an historical fact, that Christ granted Peter authority to teach and govern the whole Church, the teachers as well as the taught, although we confess he had little occasion to exercise his supreme authority, the Apostles being each and all full of the Holy Ghost and having, like Peter himself, received jurisdiction over the whole world.

II.—Christ made Peter infallible in doctrine, at least when acting as head of the Church.

1. Those of our readers who believe that *each of the Apostles* was endowed with that very same privilege, will hardly think of raising an objection against Peter being infallible when teaching the whole Church a doctrine concerning faith or morals. But this privilege of Peter in particular is so clearly expressed in the New Testament that the Holy Ghost seems to have taken care that it should be almost impossible for ordinary intelligence to deny it.

2. Christ (*a*) had *promised* that privilege to Peter, when He said to him : "Whatsoever thou shalt bind upon earth, it shall be bound also in heaven, and whatsoever thou shalt loose on earth, it shall be loosed also in heaven" (Matt. xvi. 19). For if our Lord promises to ratify in heaven some of the actions of

---

[1] Against Jovinian, bk. I, no. 26. Migne.
[2] Sermo 4 in Natal. Ord. Migne. Cf. tom. i. of Manachius, Augsburg, Bolling, 1812 ; Raynaudus, Corona aurea super mithram Rom. Pontificis.

Peter, it is evident that those actions cannot be wrong; and since He "binds" what Peter "binds," at least when acting as the head of the Church, it is evident that Peter will never bind the Church to do wrong or to believe error; in other words, Christ will always preserve him from commanding the whole Church to do anything wrong, to omit anything right, to believe anything false or to deny anything true. Therefore the text just quoted implies a promise of infallibility, which Christ has certainly fulfilled, for it is an absolute, and not a conditional promise.

In reality, the infallibility of Peter was already implied in the words: "The gates of hell shall not prevail against it" (the Church) (Matt. xvi. 18). For if error, one of the powers of hell, could prevail against the head, it would soon prevail against the Church itself, since all are bound to accept the teaching of Peter (p. 64).

This privilege was also implied in our Lord's promise that He would give him the keys, i.e., full authority over the kingdom of heaven, over the Church; for this authority is identical with that which was granted to Peter when our Lord said to him: "Whatsoever thou shalt bind upon earth, it shall be bound also in heaven" (Matt. xvi. 19), and this, we have just said, was a promise of infallibility (p. 68).

(*b*) Christ *kept His word* and made Peter the head of the Church and consequently rendered him infallible, when He said: "Feed My sheep .... feed My lambs" (John xxi. 15 and seq.). For He then bade him feed the pastors and the faithful, i.e., give them the food of religious truth; at the same time He imposed upon the pastors and the faithful the obligation of accepting his teaching, just as lambs and sheep follow their shepherds and are guided and fed by them. But from this it evidently follows that Peter cannot lead them astray and give them the poison of error instead of the wholesome food of truth: for Christ could not bind men to accept Peter's teaching, if this teaching could ever, even once, be erroneous; He would on the contrary allow the sheep and lambs to guide or desert their shepherd, should ever the guidance of the latter be unsafe. Therefore the fact that they have to accept Peter's teaching without any right to reject or discuss it, and that they must behave as sheep toward their shepherd, is a clear proof of Peter's infallibility at least when acting as the shepherd, as the head of the Church, i.e. when teaching the whole Church. On the eve of His passion, Christ was still more explicit. He told His Apostles that He had prayed that Peter's faith might not fail, and He bade him kindly confirm his brethren, when required, that they might be able to resist the persevering attacks and efforts of Satan (Matt. xvi. 18; Luke xxii. 31): " Simon, Simon, behold Satan hath desired to have you that he may sift you as wheat. But I have prayed for thee that thy faith fail not; and thou, being once converted, confirm thy brethren" (Luke xxii. 31, 32). Since Christ prayed that Peter's faith might not fail, it is obvious, first, that his and the other Apostles' faith was to be endangered owing to Satan's attacks; and since, after praying that his faith might not fail, Christ tells him to confirm the others, it is clear that what he has to confirm is their faith, and that his own faith will not fail: for if his faith can fail, if, in other words, he is not infallible, he cannot effectually confirm his brethren, as they cannot feel certain that his view is the right one unless they are persuaded that he cannot teach error. We were told by Christ that the gates of hell should not prevail against the Church, however violently Satan should attack it, because it was built on Peter; here we are told also that Satan means to attack the teachers, but that his efforts will be in vain, because Peter will confirm them. In the first case we have an allegory, in which Peter is compared to a rock; here we have the plain assertion that Satan's attack will not cause him to lose his faith, and that he will always be able to confirm that of his brethren by his infallible teaching, thus acting as the rock that keeps the building one and firm.

Though Peter was not expected to act as the rock of faith while Christ was still on earth, there is no proof that he ever lost his faith during the Passion; his will gave way and prevented him from confessing it, but it is probable that, even then, he preserved it. After Christ had left this world, we do not say that he ever actually confirmed the Apostles in the faith; for, according to tradition, Christ made each of these infallible; but his being constituted the rock, and told to confirm his brethren, shows that Christ intended him to guide and confirm in the faith any individual teacher not endowed with the same privilege of infallibility, and thus to be the means of preserving the whole Church from error in the faith. In other words, the cause of the infallibility of the Church and of her doctors is Christ; and the instrument is Peter, the rock of faith; the Apostles are the only ones whose teaching was not made infallible through Peter.[1]

3. Facts and texts which will be found below (p. 73, seq.) show that, in the early centuries, the *Bishop of Rome* was looked upon as infallible from the fact that he was Peter's successor in that see.[2] This evidently implies the belief that Peter had at least the same power finally—and therefore infallibly—to settle all points of doctrine.

Consequently we may state as a conclusion that the Church, in the time of the apostles and as it is presented to us in the New Testament, was a society under one infallible head, and composed of teachers (one of whom, Peter, was individually infallible, the others being infallible at least as a body), and of people who were taught and over each of whom Peter had full and complete authority.

Many are willing to acknowledge these privileges of Peter, but deny that it was the will of Christ that His chosen apostle should have successors in his office, endowed with the privileges and prerogatives vouchsafed to him. Against these history proves that Christ meant His Church to have, until the end of time, one visible and infallible head, with full and plenary jurisdiction over the teachers as well as the taught; in other words, it shows that Christ ordained that Peter should have successors who should enjoy his prerogatives.

III.—Christ meant Peter to have successors till the end of time as head of the Church.

1. At first sight we might question the correctness of the view we have just expressed, and think that these prerogatives (supremacy and infallibility) were granted to Peter as a personal reward for his faith and love, but were not reserved for his successors,—just as the privilege of infallibility

---

[1] Cf. Palmieri, pp. 654-657.
[2] Cf. below St. Peter Chrysologus (p. 74), Theodoret (p. 82), Innocent I. (83), Gelasius (p. 84), St. Prosper (p. 85). "If any case of extreme difficulty should arise," writes St. Patrick in 450, "let it be referred to the see of the Irish, that is of Patrick; but if it cannot be easily decided in that see . . . . we have decreed that it be sent to the Apostolic See, that is to the Chair of the apostle Peter, who holds the authority of the city of Rome" (Moran's Essays).

and universal jurisdiction over the whole world were, according to tradition, granted to each apostle as a personal prerogative and privilege, but not meant for their successors. The point is to know if the prerogatives enjoyed by one man are or are not essential to the society's nature and existence; for, if they are, they will be enjoyed by one man as long as the society remains, or is expected to remain, identically the same. In an elective monarchy, for example, there is one man having authority over all; his being chosen and appointed may be a reward of his merits, a personal favour done to him, but the existence of a king is an essential element of that form of society called an elective monarchy; should it cease to be placed under one man, it would no longer be the kind of society it originally was.

Now, *(a)* from what we saw in the last paragraph, Christ undoubtedly *made His Church a monarchical society*, since He gave Peter authority over all her members. Therefore unless we have proofs that Christ meant His Church to grow into a society essentially different from what He made her, we must conclude that he meant her to remain a monarchical society.

(b) As a matter of fact, we have one very good reason to think that He did not mean her to become essentially different; for we know that He wishes all the members of that society to have and preserve *one and the same faith;* and we have seen above (p. 41), that unless there is a head over the teachers and the taught, unity of faith is utterly impossible.

(c) But we have more than this negative reason to maintain that Christ meant His Church to remain essentially the same till the end of time.

When telling the apostles to go and teach all nations, He was speaking to *a body* of men *with a head* over them. Now the body *was to last for ever;* therefore we can have no doubt but that its head was also to last for ever.

Besides, He called His Church a kingdom, a house, a fold, and each of *these names implies a visible head.* Of this fold He said that He wished all men to enter it; therefore it is evident that He wills that fold, with its visible head, to exist till the end of time.

Of that same Church He said that the *gates of hell should not prevail* against her; and by the gates of hell He meant, as we explained above, the powers of hell, hell itself, in a word, Satan. But hell would be prevailing against her, if it could ever deprive her of her head, that most vital part, without which unity of faith would not be possible. Hence we affirm that even death, the work of sin and hell (Rom. vi. 23) will not deprive the Church of her head, which implies that, when Peter dies, a successor will be appointed to him, to be in turn succeeded by another, and so on until the end of time, i.e., as long as the Church exists.

2. According to St. Paul, the Church is a body, the head of which cannot say to the feet, "I have no need of you" (1 Cor. xii, 12, 21). But if there be no other head than Christ, the *words of St. Paul are not true*, for Christ has need of no one. Therefore there is another head besides Christ, and since St. Paul speaks in general, there will be a head in the Church as long as she is a body, as long as she exists.

3. But do we not put a wrong construction on our Lord's and St. Paul's words? We think not; for *those who lived nearer to the times of the apostles*, and had consequently every opportunity of knowing what the apostles, and therefore Christ, did really teach and mean, understood them in the sense that we do; they believed that Peter was to have successors in his office of head of the Church, and this alone, independently of what we read in the New Testament, shows what they were taught to believe.

(a) During the early centuries, as well as later on, the *Bishop of Rome* was distinctly called the *successor of Peter*, his see the *See of Peter*, the *Apostolic See*. St. Cyprian, for example, (+ 258) says that Pope Cornelius is sitting "in the see of Peter."[1] Firmilian writes that the Pope boasts of his title of "Successor of Peter" (Epist. 75, inter Epist. Cyp.); St. Optatus (+ 370), to confute the Donatists, refers them to the "Apostolic Chair of Peter, in which one chair unity is preserved by all . . . . so that whosoever should set up another chair would be at once a schismatic and a sinner, assuming sacrilegiously the keys of the kingdom of heaven, sacrilegiously fighting against the Chair of Peter by his presumption and audacity;"[2] St. Jerome (+ 420) writes to Pope Damasus: "I solicit from the pastor help for the sheep; I am linked in communion with Your Blessedness, i.e., with

---

[1] Patr. Lat. Epist. 52, ad Antonian.   [2] De Schism. Donat. ii. 2-5.

the Chair of Peter; I know that the Church is built on it.... I am speaking to the successor of the fisherman;"[1] St. Peter Chrysologus (+ 450), writing to Eutyches, tells him to apply to the Pope, "since Peter, who still lives and presides in his Chair, gives the truth to those who are seeking it."[2] Pope Gelasius and the Councils of Arles and Ephesus use the same expressions (pp. 77, 85). Now to our mind, the mere fact that the Bishop of Rome alone is called Peter's successor, and his see the See of Peter, the Apostolic See, supposes the belief that the Bishop of Rome enjoyed the prerogatives of Peter, viz., his supremacy over the whole Church (and his infallibility), and consequently the belief that Peter was to have successors as head of the Church. For the bishop of Antioch, though also his successor in that see, was not spoken of as Peter's successor, nor his see as "the see of Peter," the "Apostolic" see; nor was the see of Jerusalem called an "Apostolic" see: this shows that the Bishop of Rome alone inherited *all* the prerogatives of his predecessor in the eyes of the early Christians and therefore was looked upon as the head of the Church; while no other bishop was endowed with all the prerogatives (for example, the universal jurisdiction) of his predecessor.

(b) Indeed some of the writers we have just quoted, viz., St. Optatus and St. Peter Chrysologus, tell us explicitly that they regard the Bishop of Rome as the *head of the Church*, as well as Peter's successor in his see; and other writers are just as explicit, nay, even more so. Tertullian (160-240), for instance, writes that the Bishop of the Romans considered himself and was considered by others as "bishop of bishops" and as the head of the Church;[3] St. Athanasius (+ 373), archbishop of Alexandria, "the hero of his age," says Boehringer, writes to the Pope: "You and your predecessors, the apostolic rulers, have been placed at the head and commanded to take care of all the Churches, that you might come to our help."[4] St. Cyril of Alexandria (+ 444) calls Peter the prince and head of the apostles, and his successor, St. Celestine, "the archbishop of the whole world."[5] Theodoret (+ 458) writes: "I pray you to persuade the Archbishop Leo to use his apostolic authority .... for that

[1] St. Hier. Epist. 15 ad Damasum.   [2] Epist. ad Eutych. Bib. Max.
[3] Pudicit. I. Rigalt.   [4] Epist. ad Felicem P.
[5] Hom. xi., Enc. in S. Deipar.

holy See holds the helm of all the Churches in the world" (in Epist. ad Renat). "That Church," says St. Augustine (+ 430), "even by the acknowledgement of the human race, from the Apostolic See through the succession of bishops .... has held the summit of authority; .... to be unwilling to give her the first place is surely either the highest impiety or headlong arrogance;"[1] and he calls the Pope "the pastor of the whole Church,"[2] and "the pastor of pastors."[3]

(c) The belief in the supremacy of the Pope is manifested by the numerous *appeals* made to him, such being sent only to a superior. Privatus, condemned by St. Cyprian, has recourse to him, as also St. Denys, the patriarch of Alexandria, in 263.[4] In 313 Constantine appeals to Pope Melchiades on behalf of Cecilian, bishop of Carthage, accused by Donatus. St. John Chrysostom (347-407), patriarch of Constantinople, writes to Pope Innocent I.: "I beseech you to write that all that was so unjustly done (his deposition) is of no value, and that those who acted so wrongly should be subjected to the pains of the ecclesiastical law."[5] Flavian, archbishop of Constantinople in 449, and Theodoret (+ 458), also sent appeals to Rome; so did the Eusebians (in the quarrel with Marcel of Ancyra, St. Athanasius and Asclepas of Gaza,[6]) and even heretics, as the Novatists (252), Pelagius (in 417), Nestorius (in 417), and Eutyches (in 448); and we see St. Ambrose (+ 397) recommending the schismatics of Antioch to bring the affair to Rome,[7] and St. Basil (+ 379), giving an advice to the same effect to the patriarch of Alexandria, St. Athanasius. The right of appeal to Rome, says St. Augustine[8] existed before the Council of Nicea; and Leo the Great, in the controversy with St. Hilary of Arles,[9] calls it an ancient custom.

(d) The *prominent part* taken by the Popes in the *early Councils* points to the same belief, for the bishops never protested against their pretensions. The Popes presided directly or through their legates over the eastern Councils of Nicea (325), Sardica (347), Ephesus (431), Chalcedon (451); they

---

[1] De Utilit. Credend. viii. no. 35.   [2] In l. 2 contra Faust. c. 7.
[3] In l. 4 contra 2 episc. Pelag. c. 12   [4] Euseb. H. E. vii. 9.
[5] Patr. Gr. li., lii., col. 532, 534-536.
[6] Cf. Athanasius, Apolog. contra Arian. n. 20; Julii epist. ad Euseb. n. 2 and 20; Theodoret. H.E. l. 2, c. 20.
[7] Epist. 56, Theophil. no. 4, 7.   [8] Epist. 43, no. 7.   [9] Epist. 10.

sent to the Fathers who sat in these and the other General Councils, orders or directions which were complied with ; they sanctioned their decrees, if they were satisfied with them (see p. 86). Socrates and Sozomen, Greek historians, tell us that in the East no council could be held without the Pope's consent, under pain of nullity.[1] "It is a sacerdotal law," says Sozomen,[2] "that the things done contrary to the decree of the Bishop of the Romans be looked on as null." "The ecclesiastical rule," writes Socrates,[3] "expressly commands that the Churches shall not make any ordinance without the sanction of the Bishop of Rome."

(e) Indeed this supremacy was *asserted by the Popes* as a right, and not even Firmilian called their claim an arrogant assumption, though, to use his own expression, Pope Stephen "boasted of the pre-eminence of his see," would pay no heed to "the bishops who, from all parts, were asking him to change his determination," and "forbade the whole Church to communicate with Cyprian."[4] No one protests when in the first century St. Clement (67-76 or 92-101) tells the Corinthians "to obey the things" he has written.[5] In the second century, St. Irenæus (+202) respectfully asks Pope St. Victor not to excommunicate certain Asiatic bishops, as he intended to do ; but he does not deny that he has the right of excommunicating them. In the third century, St. Cyprian remarks that "the Pope uses his authority to make the African bishops accept a strange tradition,"[6] but he does not refuse to grant that the Pope has authority over all (see p. 89, foot note). We find no protest when, in the fourth century, Pope Julius (+341) declares that "there is an ecclesiastical rule that the Churches should not make synodal laws or ordinances, without the consent of the Bishop of Rome ;"[7] or when Pope Damasus in 370 furnishes St. Athanasius, thrust out by the Arian party, with letters asserting his right to restore him to his patriarchal see ; "[8] or when he declares that he holds the chief helm of the Church.[9] The language of a superior is spoken by Pope Siricius to the

[1] Socr. H.E. ii. 2 ; Sozom. H.E. iii. 7.   [2] H.E. iii. 10.   [3] H.E. ii. 8
[4] Epist. 17 ; Inter Epist. Cypr., Epist. 75. Edit. Ben.
[5] Epist. ci. 47, 57, 58, (Gallandi) a letter in which, as Dr. Lightfoot, late bishop of Durham, says (On St. Clement's Epistle 398), "the Pope assumes such an authoritative tone."
[6] Epist. ad Pompeium 74, Patr. Lat. iii. col. 1128, and seq.
[7] Socr. H. E. iii. 10.   [8] Socr. H. E. iv. 37.
[9] Epist. 5, Prosp. Labbe, ii. 876-882.

bishops of Tarragona in 386 ;[1] by Pope Innocent in 410 to the bishop of Rouen,[2] to Macedonia,[3] to the bishop of Gubbio,[4] and to the council of Milevis.[5] To the bishop of Carthage he says that the whole authority of the episcopate is derived from the Apostolic See, and affirms that, according to the Fathers, no local action should be counted as completed until the entire sentence is confirmed by the authority of his See.[6] Pope Zozimus (+422) writes to the Council of Carthage : " The tradition of the Fathers attributes so much authority to the Apostolic See that no one could question its judgment . . . our authority is such that no one can refuse to stand by our decision."[7] " All the Church knows," says Pope Gelasius (+496), " that the See of Peter has a right to judge the whole Church and cannot be judged by any one . . . no one is allowed to appeal from it . . :"[8] At the beginning of the fifth century the right of the Popes to send vicars apostolic through the various parts of the world, with the mission to carry out Papal instructions, was looked upon as according to ancient custom.[9] The fact that such explicit claims to supreme authority are listened to by the Church throughout the early centuries is a clear proof that from the beginning she universally considered the Pope as her head.

(*f*) Far from protesting against the Pope's interference or claims to supremacy, St. Basil (+379) asks Pope Damasus[10] to remedy the evils that afflict the Eastern Church, to visit it himself or through some delegates, to set matters right in Cesarea, and to determine who ought and who ought not to be held in communion. Even *Councils* proclaim in unmistakable terms the belief of the teaching Church in the Pope's supremacy. As early as 314 the Fathers of the Council of Arles write that in the See of Rome " the Apostles continue to sit in judgment," and they send their deliberations to the Pope " that they may be made known to all by him who holds the mightiest diocese."[11] The discipline invoked by Pope Julius, writing to the Eastern bishops, and other circumstances

---

[1] Galland. vii. pp. 533-534.   [2] Gall. viii. 547.
[3] ib. 575.   [4] ib. 586.   [5] ib. 602-603.
[6] Epist. 29 ib. 599. Cf. Lindsay's Evidence of the Papacy, pp. 214-232.
[7] Conc. tom. ii. p. 1572.   [8] Epist. 13 ad episc. Dardaniæ. Labbe, iv. 1200, 1203.
[9] Cf. Thomass. Vetus et Nova disciplina pars i. lib. i. cc. 30, 51.
[10] In Epist. 70. Migne.   [11] Labbe i. 1425-6.

point out that a synodal letter was sent by the Council of Nicea (325) to Pope Sylvester, and that its decrees were confirmed by him.[1] The Council of Sardica (347) expressly approved of the Pope's conduct with regard to the cause of Athanasius and of the other bishops, and sanctioned the right of appeal to Rome. The Council of Ephesus (431) declares that it merely obeys the Pope (see p. 85). At Chalcedon (451) the Fathers hear, without protestation, these words of the legate, Paschasinus : "We have in our hands the orders of the most blessed and Apostolic man, the Pope of the city of Rome, which is the head of all the Churches" (Act. i.) ; and they themselves say that "All the primacy and chief honour are preserved, according to the canons, to the most beloved archbishop of old Rome" (Act xvi.) ; nay more, they will write to the Pope : "We ask you to honour our judgment with your decrees, and just as we agree with the head, we ask you to do what your sons wish." Their own decrees were ratified by the Pope, with the exception of the twenty-eighth, which had been passed by only one-third of the Fathers. In the fifth Œcumenical Council, the second of Constantinople (553), everything points to the great authority of Pope Vigilius and to its recognition by the Fathers.[2] In the sixth Œcumenical Council, third of Constantinople (681), they entirely leave to the Pope's decision what should be done, thus confessing both his supremacy and infallibility.[3]

It is a fact which no one denies that *from the sixth century and upwards* the Bishop of Rome acted and was looked upon as one having full and plenary jurisdiction both over the teachers and the laity, so that, even if we had no documents from the earlier centuries, the fact alluded to would of itself show that the first Christians looked upon him as the head of the Church, for no other hypothesis could account for the belief of the Church in the sixth. Nay more, this belief of the early Church proves two points conclusively, first, that the Apostles and our Lord taught that Peter was to have *successors* with the same full and plenary jurisdiction he had himself ; secondly, that Peter and his fellow-Apostles declared that the *Bishop of Rome* was to be considered as Peter's successor and

---

[1] Cf. Wouters, Hist. Eccl. compend. i. p. 182, no. 2.
[2] Cf. Darras, Hist. de l'Eglise, vol. xiv. pp. 525, and seq.
[3] in Epist. Syn.

head of the Church ; for that belief of the first Christians has to be accounted for, and, as we shall see at the end of this chapter, no other cause can be assigned to it.

We must here observe that in those early centuries we have not merely witnesses of the Apostles' teaching ; we hear the doctrine actually held out and *taught by the authorised* propagators of the faith themselves, of whom we said above that they were *infallible* as a body. Now that body, in the sixth century and previously, teaches that Christ meant Peter to have successors as the head of His fold, and that the Bishop of Rome is his successor and enjoys as such full and plenary jurisdiction over the whole Church. Therefore we may look upon it as an undeniable *truth* that Christ intended His whole flock to be under the jurisdiction, control and guidance of one man. For an infallible teaching body could not have taught, as it did both explicitly and implicitly, that Christ willed His Church to be a monarchy, if in reality He had in view that she should be a republic or an oligarchy ; it could not have taught error on such an essential point as the very constitution of the Church, have undone the work of Christ, deprived the successors of the Apostles of their independence, and declared at the same time that this was the very thing Christ had in view. [1]

IV.—Christ meant Peter's successors to be infallible in matters of doctrine.

We added that Christ intended Peter's successors to possess a privilege of immunity from error in religious matters.

1. The fact that Peter was made infallible in order that he might confirm his brethren in the faith implies that his infallibility was not merely a personal favour (p. 71), but that he was invested with it as head of the Church, and consequently that this prerogative was intended to pass on to his successors till the end of time. It would seem *strange* that

---

[1] The reader will observe that our conclusion is independent of the solution given to the questions : Was Peter ever in Rome ? Did he die in Rome ? Was he at least Bishop of Rome ? though many of the quotations we make, prove that the early centuries would have given them an affirmative answer (see Dr. Leclerc, de Rom. S. Petri Episc., Louvain, 1888 ; Jaugey's Dict. Apolog. pp. 2393-2456, Delhomme and Briguet, Paris ; Livius's St. Peter Bishop of Rome, Burns and Oates, London.)

Christ, who actually prayed that His disciples might be one, should have provided His Church with the means of preserving unity of faith (p. 68) when, each Apostle being infallible, there was less danger of division, and should have allowed her to be deprived of it when the need of it became more urgent, namely, when her children grew more numerous, when heretics waged war against her, and when the first Apostles were no more. Therefore we may rightly infer that Peter's privilege of infallibility was not a personal one, meant to end with him, but an essential prerogative granted to the head of the teaching body.

2. However we have more direct proofs that Christ's intention was that the chief of His fold should be infallible until the end of time. We know for certain that *error cannot prevail* against the Church (p. 58); from this it follows, 1°, that the faithful cannot be commanded by their head to believe error; 2°, that the supreme Pastor as such must teach the truth, as error would prevail if he could possibly preach and command all to accept a spurious doctrine. We cannot object that in such a case he has no right to command, for we have just seen (p. 71) that the head of the Church has full and plenary jurisdiction over her, the very same authority that Peter had and which we have described as that of a shepherd over his sheep, an authority therefore that the flock has no right to reject or even to question (p. 64).

3. But since the pastors and the faithful are *bound to accept his guidance and teaching*, whenever the successor of Peter chooses to speak as head of the Church, that is, as supreme shepherd, it evidently follows that in such cases he cannot set forth an erroneous doctrine, not only because error and the gates of hell would then soon prevail against the Church, but because if the head could teach error, it would follow that Christ in binding us to obey and believe him, binds us eventually to believe a falsehood, which of course is impossible.

No doubt, the fact that our Lord obliges us to submit to the commands of a superior is not a proof that such commands are just and right, although so long as a superior does not demand that we should do evil, there may be merit in submitting to his orders; but His binding us to obey when we are enjoined to believe (and this He does, since He gives the head full authority to bind and loose, pp. 71, 64), implies that we can never be obliged to believe what is untrue and that the head of the Church can never in that quality teach what is false. "It would be foolish to say," writes Cardinal Newman, when yet a Protestant, in one of his Oxford tracts, "that the Church [say 'the head of the Church'] has authority to declare dogmatical points and yet that she can err. How can the Church have authority, if she is not certainly true in her declarations? Should we say that she has authority to tell a lie? Dogmatical matters are not, like things of earthly interest, grounded on material expediency which is to be determined by discretion. Dogmatical matters appeal to conscience, and conscience is only subject to truth in matters of belief. To say that the Church has authority, and yet that she may err in her declarations, would be to destroy the authority of conscience, which every one should hold sacred ; it would be to substitute something else besides truth, as sovereign lord of conscience, which would be tyranny. If the Church has authority in dogmatical matters, she must be the organ and representation of truth. Her teaching must be identified with truth : in one word, the Church must be infallible."

4. When our Lord was addressing the Apostles and telling them to go and teach all nations, adding that He would be with them to the end of time (Matt. xxviii. 18-20), He was speaking to a *body of men* placed *under one infallible head*. We may therefore conclude that the body addressed by Him is not only meant to last to the end of time (p. 55), but to remain identically the same, viz., a body of teachers under one infallible head, till the consummation of ages. Indeed such must be our conclusion, unless we have a distinct statement from our Lord or His Apostles that Christ wishes to baffle human reason and deprive the body of teachers of those means to preserve unity of faith, which reason considers to be most suitable and which Christ Himself had at first appointed (p. 68). But far from meeting any such statement in the Bible or in the writings of those who lived nearer to the apostolic times, we have, apart from the texts already quoted, most convincing proofs that Christ and His Apostles taught the contrary, viz., that the head of the Church, Peter's successor, would be, like him, endowed with a privilege of infallibility.

5. We have the evidence that *in the early centuries the Bishop of Rome* was not only regarded as the head of the Church, but acted and was looked upon as infallible. No doubt, we do not find the word "infallibility," but under

simple modes of expression, the very same doctrine was recognised and acted upon from the first. It is implied in what the early writers say of the faith and doctrine of the Roman Bishop; but above all in the fact that all matters of faith were referred to him; that there was no appeal from his decision; that questions of belief were considered as definitely settled when he had decided them; that Councils obeyed his directions even in matters of doctrine and asked for his sanction; that individuals and Churches had to believe what the Pope believed; that when a man's doctrine was approved by him, it was held as orthodox; and that no one protested against his claims to decide all points of belief without appeal. As a matter of fact, a Council did all but proclaim his infallibility.

a. Surely the following *assertions imply credence* in the infallibility of the Bishop of Rome: St. Cyprian (+ 258) writes to Pope Cornelius that "they [the Schismatics] have dared to cross the seas and apply to the See of Peter and to the chief [or ruling] Church . . . without thinking that those to whom they apply are the Romans whose faith was so highly praised by the Apostle and to whom heretical perfidy cannot gain access."[1] In an angry letter to Pompeius, he says that "up to that day the Roman Bishop had been the channel between Christ and the Church, distributing to all the divine teaching," although he adds that the channel wants repair.[2] St. Gregory Nazianzen (+ 390), in his poem "de Vita Sua" (v. 562 seq.), compares Rome to Constantinople, and of the former he says that she has always had the right faith, as becomes her who presides over all; of the latter he declares that she lies in the depth of perdition. According to St. Augustine (+ 430) the Pope's words speak the faith clearly and unhesitatingly: "In the words of the Apostolic See the Catholic Faith is so sure and so clear . . . that no one is allowed to have doubts about it."[3] According to St. Peter Chrysologus (+ 450), "Peter, who lives and presides in his own Chair, gives the true faith to those who seek it" from the Roman Pontiff.[4] Theodoret (+ 458) writes that the See of Peter has always been preserved from heresy[5] and he says to Leo: "Your see is adorned with

[1] Epist. 55 ad Cornel. Ed. Bened.
[2] Epist. xxiv. ad Pompeium; see below, answer to objections from St. Cyprian's writings, p. 89.
[3] St. Aug. Epist. 157.
[4] Epist. ad Eutych. inter Acta Concil. Chalced.
[5] Epist. ad Renatum presbyt., Epist. 116, edit. Migne.

many prerogatives . . . above all faith adorns it . . . their [the Apostles,] God has also glorified their see by placing your Reverence in it to diffuse the rays of the true faith."[1]

b. All *matters of faith*, we said, *were referred to the Roman Bishop*. St. Irenaeus writes that the "Holy Roman Church . . the mistress of all the churches must be consulted in all doubts about faith or morals."[2] Accordingly we see St. Cyril of Alexandria asking the Pope what he is to do with Nestorius : "It is a long established usage to make known such matters [questions of doctrine] to your Holiness. But it is necessary that your Holiness's judgment be made known also to the bishops of Macedonia and the East."[3] "You know," writes Innocent I. in 410 to the Fathers of the Council of Milevis, "that throughout all the provinces, answers to questions always emanate from the Apostolic spring, specially as often as matters of faith are under discussion. I am of opinion that all our brethren and fellow bishops ought simply to refer to Peter." We hear of no protestation against such a claim; on the contrary, the Fathers of the second Council of Constantinople, (5th Œcumenical Council), thus address the Roman Bishop : "To thee, as being the bishop of the first see of the whole Church, we leave what should be done, thus standing on the firm rock of faith."[4] As we said above, appeals were made to the Pope, even before the Council of Nicea, specially concerning matters of doctrine. St. Denys of Alexandria, though a patriarch, appealed to Pope St. Denys in 263, as he was accused of inaccurate language, if not of heresy, while attacking Sabellianism.[5] Even Eutyches, condemned by a local council of Constantinople in 448, sent several documents and an act of appeal to Pope St. Leo.

c. *From the Sovereign Pontiff's decision there was no appeal;* and when the Popes remind the Church of this, we hear of no protestation. No one protests, for example, when Pope Zozimus (+ 422) writes to the Council of Carthage : "The tradition of the Fathers attributes so much authority to the

---

[1] Theodoret. Epist. 113, Migne iv. p. 1314.
[2] De Hær. lib. 3. c. 3.—cf. Schneeman, St. Iren. de Eccl. Rom. principatu testimonium, Friburg, 1870.
[3] Epist. 8. Cœlestin. n. 1, 7. Galland. t. 9.
[4] In Epist. Syn.
[5] Euseb. H. E. vii. 9.

Apostolic See that no one could ever question its judgment... our authority is such that no one can refuse to stand by our decision;"[1] or when Pope Gelasius I. (+ 496) says: "The entire Church knows that the See of Peter has the right to loose what has been bound by no matter whom: because that see has a right to judge the whole Church and cannot be judged by any one, for, according to the canons, it can receive appeals from every part of the world, while no one may appeal from it," and he adds: "Following the custom of the past, the Apostolic See has often, without the presence of any synod, absolved those who had been unjustly condemned, and has condemned even without synods, those who had deserved it."[2] Pope Celestine (+ 430) writes to the bishops of Gaul: "It was necessary diligently to enquire what the rulers of the Roman Church had judged regarding the heresy... and what they had decided should be adhered to."[3] No one protests against these claims of the Popes to decide without appeal; and we need hardly observe that this right of theirs is spoken of as an "ancient custom." Indeed we see it explicitly recognised by the Council of Sardica (A.D. 347) at the end of the seventh canon about the appellants: "If the Pope is of opinion that the bishops [of the province or neighbourhood] are not sufficient to terminate the matter, let him act as he shall determine according to his own most wise judgment."[4]

d. Not only were there no appeals from the Pope's decision, but moreover, once decided by him causes were considered as ended, and *questions of faith as definitely settled.* Now this could hardly have been the case, if his decisions had not been deemed infallible. St. Augustine says, in his second sermon after the letter of Pope Innocent I. had been received in Africa: "We have already sent two councils to the Apostolic See on the subject, and answers have come: the cause is ended; may the error also end!"[5] Speaking elsewhere of two letters of the Pelagians, he says:

[1] Conc. t. 2. p. 1572.
[2] Epist. 13 ad Episc. Dardaniæ. Labbe. iv.
[3] As related by Vincent of Lerins, in Migne, vol. 50, p. 528; cf ibid. p. 607, letter of Sixtus to John, bishop of Antioch.
[4] Labbe, Concil. t. ii. col. 659.
[5] Sermo 131. Edit. Ben.

"the letters of Pope Innocent have done away with all doubt on the subject" discussed in those letters.¹ Sozomen relates that, when Pope Damasus had written to the eastern Churches on the question of the Trinity, "All kept silent, because the judgment of the Roman Church had ended the controversy."² St. Prosper (+ 455) shows how that same heresy of the Pelagians had been "put down:" "we are firm and sure on the point," he says, because it was condemned by two Pontiffs—and this they did without an Œcumenical council—and by one Pontiff at the Council of Ephesus. "Their [the Pelagians'] arms were destroyed when Innocent . . . struck them with the Apostolic sword and called a Council of the bishops of Palestine . . . and when Pope Zozimus confirmed the decrees of the African bishops, and put in their hands the sword of Peter, and also when Pope Celestine helped Cyril of Alexandria . . . with the apostolic sword against the Nestorians and again put down the Pelagians, whose heresy had something in common with them."³ In the eyes of Prosper, the Popes have done almost everything.

Even Councils consider the question settled, once the Pope has spoken. At the third Œcumenical Council, that of Ephesus (431), composed of about two hundred bishops and presided over by St. Cyril who represented Pope Celestine, sentence of deposition was passed on Nestorius by the Fathers, who declared that they were "necessarily constrained by the canons and by the letter of our most holy Father and fellow-minister Celestine, the Bishop of the Church of Rome." And, speaking still more explicity, Firmus, bishop of Cappadocia, one of the legates, rose and said: "The Apostolic See of Celestine has decided the affair and has pronounced sentence upon it before, in the letter addressed to Cyril of Alexandria . . . in accordance with which sentence and in furtherance thereof, we have pronounced the canonical judgment against Nestorius." And the Fathers added that, having read that he had also condemned Pelagius, Celestius, and others, they themselves held them as condemned.⁴ The Pope had spoken, for them the question was settled.

¹ Contra duas Epist. Pel.Lib. 2. c. 3.   ² H.E. vi. c. 22.
³ Adv. collat. c. 21.   ⁴ Mansi t. iv. col. 1123, 1155-1181, 1295; Epist. ad. Cyril. in Conc. Ephes. Labbe iii. col. 878-879.

e. As a matter of fact, the first eight Œcumenical *Councils* either got their decrees *confirmed* by the Pope (Nicea in 325, Sardica in 347, the 5th Œcumenical in 550, the 8th in 869); or simply *carried out his instructions* in condemning what he had already condemned (Ephesus in 431, the 7th Œcumenical in 786); or did both one and the other, that is to say, obeyed his directions and asked him to confirm their decrees (1st of Constantinople in 381, Chalcedon in 451, 6th Œcum. in 681). Now Pope Nicholas I., in a letter read at the eighth Œcumenical Council (Act. iv.), tells us why the Bishop of Rome's sanction is asked : " No conclusion can be arrived at without the consent of . . . the Roman Pontiff . . . the authority and sanction of the Roman Church corroborates all Synods and holy Councils and gives them their firmness." In other words, the decrees of a Council are not irrevocable and cannot claim the assent of faith, unless they have received the consent and sanction of the Roman Pontiff. This accounts for a letter sent to the Pope by the emperor Marcian, asking that he should signify to him by letter that he had ratified the decrees of the Council of Chalcedon, because the partisans of Eutyches maintained that he had not confirmed them.[1] That Pope Celestine meant his directions to be binding is clear from what he writes to his legates at *Ephesus*: " We command that the authority of the Apostolic See shall be respected . . . If there be any discussion, you must stand as judges of what is said, but you must not allow any one to attack you,—vos de eorum sententiis judicare debeatis, non subire certamen "[2] We have seen above (p. 85) how the Fathers of Ephesus acted according to the Pope's directions. St. Leo writes to the Council of *Chalcedon*,[3] that he will preside through his legates, so that " enabled to know what we believe, you may feel sure of what we wish." And to make them understand that they are bound to conform to his belief, he adds that they must decide according to what he wrote to Bishop Flavian. When, at the Council, some question as to whether the view of Flavian on the subject be orthodox, all doubt vanishes as soon as Paschasinus, the legate, answers : " Flavian has given a holy, complete, and catholic exposition of the faith; for his

[1] Epist. 110, inter Epist. S. Leonis. [2] Epist. 17 Cœlestini penes Constant. [3] Ep. ad Conc. Chalc. p. 71. Labbe iv.

exposition of the faith is in conformity with the letters of the most blessed and Apostolic man, the Roman Pope" (Act. i.) Later on, the Fathers being asked to declare the doctrines of their faith openly and fully, give this answer : " what has been said [by the Pope] is enough ; we cannot make a different exposition . . . such is our belief ; no one of us has any doubt on the subject; we have already signed the letter of the Pope. (Act 2). At the 6*th* Œ*cumenical* Council (681), a letter from Pope Agatho is read, in which, after giving the doctrine of Peter, the Pontiff says that the doctrine and "authority of the Roman Church is the one which the whole Church, the general synods and doctors, have always followed in all things;" and though this was a clear hint that the Fathers were also to follow Agatho's teaching as the sure and immutable rule of faith, far from protesting against such pretentions, the Fathers listened and heartily approved of the statement (Act. 4 and 18); nay, as we have already said, they wrote to Agatho and told him that they "left everything in the hands of him who stands on the firm rock of faith." But if it is true that the whole Church has always listened to and followed the doctrinal authority of the Roman Bishop, it is evident that she looked upon him as infallible, as otherwise she would have undoubtedly at some time or other followed some other pastor: we should not always and in everything be guided by one and the same teacher, if we had some other means, equally safe, of finding truth or of avoiding error.

Therefore from the fact that the early Œcumenical Councils obeyed the directions of the Pope, or procured his sanction to their decrees, we may conclude that, in the eyes of the primitive Church, the full and supreme authority to define matters of faith did not reside in a *majority* of bishops, all equal to one another, since the vote of one—the Bishop of Rome—could annul a decree, and the majority, nay even the unanimity of the bishops could define nothing without his sanction. We may also conclude that full and supreme authority to teach did not, in the eyes of the early Church, reside in the *union* of a majority of bishops with the Pope; for when the Pope spoke, the bishops felt that they could not refuse to ratify and accept his teaching, and a decree on matters of faith passed by him alone, was looked upon by them as binding, while what they themselves decided required his sanction. In the eyes of the early Councils, the supreme and infallible authority was certainly found in an *Œcumenical Council* with the Pope as its head; only it did not, in their eyes, reside in the majority, it truly resided in that one man, the Bishop of Rome, without whom no Council could be Œcumenical, to whom all had to submit, and whose sanction was necessary if their decrees concerning doctrine were to be considered irrevocable. In order that a doctrinal decision might be regarded as *conciliary*, no doubt a majority of voters in its favour was requisite; however this did not suffice when there was question of its being real and *unchangeable:* the Pope's sanction was required. But yet another conclusion forces itself upon us—and this is the point we wish to make clear—if all agreed that they had to submit to the Pope's decisions in questions of faith, it follows that they undoubtedly looked upon him as infallible in such matters.

(*f*) Now, if Councils themselves felt bound to hold the same view as the Pope with regard to doctrine, we may be sure that *individuals and particular Churches* were under the same obligation. Hence St. Irenæus (+202) writes that "With this Church, on account of her more powerful headship [or supremacy], it is necessary that every Church . . . should agree [or resort to] in which [in communion with which Church] has always been preserved the tradition which is from the Apostles."[1] But if all churches must be of one mind with the Roman Church in order to preserve the Apostles' doctrine, it follows in the opinion of St. Irenæus that this one Church cannot lose it. St. Jerome says in 414 to Demetrias: "When you were a little child and Bishop Anastasius of blessed memory ruled the Roman Church, a fierce tempest from parts of the East tried to defile the simplicity of that faith which was praised by the voice of the Apostle . . . and because I have learned that, in certain places, the venomous plants still live and put forth shoots, I think that I ought to give you this warning that you hold fast the faith of Holy Innocent, who is both the successor and the (spiritual) son of the aforesaid man and of the Apostolic Chair; nor, however prudent and wise you may seem to yourself, receive any strange doctrine."[2] A few years before, St.

---

[1] Ad. Hæres. lib. 3. c. 3.
[2] Epist. 130 ad Demetr. v. no. 16 Migne, vol. 1, p. 992.

Ambrose (+397) had also said that one must agree with the Roman Pontiff. His brother Satyrus was a bishop of doubtful faith; "he called the bishop [his brother] to him, and not accounting any grace true which was not of the true faith, he enquired of him whether he agreed with the catholic bishops, that is with the Roman Church."[1] "All those," writes St. Maximus (+662), "who confess the Lord with the right faith, look at the most Holy Roman Church and her confession and faith as the Sun of eternal light . . . she has the keys of the true faith and confession in Christ."[2] *

[1] De excessu fratris.　　[2] Opp. t. ii. p. 72 seq.

* We see it often stated that, pending the controversy about re-baptism, St. Cyprian, not to speak of his suffragans, clearly showed that he did not feel bound to accept the Pope's views, and consequently did not believe in the Pope's infallibility or even supremacy. But in order to conclude that St. Cyprian and the early centuries did not believe in the Pope's infallibility and supremacy, there remains to be proved (1) that St. Cyprian took part against the Pope on the question of re-baptism; (2) that the documents which show him to be hostile to the Pope's supremacy and infallibility are genuine and not the work of the Donatists; for Prof. Tizzani holds that they are apocryphal, in La Celebre Contesa fra S. Stefano e S. Cypriano, Salviucci, Roma, 1862; (3) that, granting the documents to be genuine, St. Cyprian looked upon the question of re-baptism as one of belief, and not of discipline; for if the evidence goes in favour of the latter view, as it does from the genuine or spurious documents we have, to reject the Pope's directions is not to deny his infallibility; (4) that in refusing to obey the Pope St. Cyprian was denying his supremacy and not merely committing an act of disobedience, which he perhaps thought was justified. As a matter of fact, we know of nothing that can show St. Cyprian to have denied the Pope's supremacy or infallibility; for his saying that no African bishop forced the African episcopate to accept his own view was probably a hint against the Pope's use of his supremacy, but it was not necessarily denying that supremacy; likewise, his saying that Christ alone could judge bishops, was not necessarily denying that He made use of the Pope or of Councils to judge them. But even granting that St. Cyprian did deny the Pope's supremacy and infallibility, what of it? Before concluding that the primitive Church did not believe in them, there still remains to be proved (5) that St. Cyprian was expressing the view of the Church at large, and not merely a private opinion, his own or that of his province. The fact that an opinion is held even by St. Cyprian and his suffragans is by no means a convincing proof that it is correct and held by the Church as a body. As an illustration of this, take the view of this same St. Cyprian on the question of re-baptism. Now we think we can sufficiently show that the primitive Church did not share St. Cyprian's views about the Pope's prerogatives, so that, even if we had no documents to prove that in the Saint's time the Church did believe in them, the fact that she believed in them at one time implies she did not deny them in St. Cyprian's; for the Church, being infallible as a

(g) When a man was *approved by the Pope, he was held to be orthodox by all*. "If the followers of Apollinarius have been judged to be orthodox by the Western Synod, which at first with Pope Damasus had condemned them, let them prove it, and we shall agree with them; for if they were accepted [as orthodox], it is evident that their doctrine was right." Such are the words of St. Gregory Nazianzen to Cledonius.[1] St. Jerome, afraid of holding communion with heretics, writes to Pope Damasus: "Meletius, Vitalis and Paulinus say that they adhere to you. If one asserted this, I could believe him; as it is, either two of them, or all three, lie   I conjure your Blessedness . . . that you would signify to me by your letters with which bishop of Syria it is my duty to hold communion."[2] If he wish not to be looked upon as a heretic," says Maximus, "let him satisfy not this one or that one, but above all, the Roman See. If this See be satisfied, all will call him pious and orthodox."[3]

(h) We have mentioned the names of several Popes who have acted and spoken as if they were infallible, nay more, who have implicitly claimed to be infallible—Innocent I., Zozimus, Gelasius, Celestine (pp. 83, 84), and we have heard the greatest doctors of the early Church implicitly confessing this prerogative—Gregory Nazianzen, Augustine, Cyril of Alexandria, etc.; we have seen even eight Œcumenical Councils falling in with the same view. But, among these Œcumenical Councils, there is one to which we beg to call the reader's attention more particularly, for in it the Pope's

body, could not teach contradictory views on one and the same point of doctrine. In conclusion, we are loath to believe that St. Cyprian held an opinion out of harmony with the Church's teaching and belief, because it is not sufficiently proved that he did, and also because it would imply inconsistency in such a man. We gave two texts above, showing his belief in the Pope's supremacy and infallibility; we might have added that, even during a vacancy of the Apostolic See, all the correspondence that took place between him and the vacancy Committee points to this belief; during the controversy he complains of the use the Pope makes of his authority (Epist. ad Pompeium 74), but he does not deny it; and we are told that he ended by admitting his error and accepting the Pope's teaching on the question of re-baptism (S. Hier. Patr. Lat. xxiii. col. 177-178; St. Aug. contra Donatist. lib. 2 no. 4; Bedæ Aliquot Quæstiones. Patr. Lat. xciii. col. 458).

[1] Epist. ad Cledon. de Apoll. sequacibus, no. 2.
[2] Epist. xvi. ad Damasum, Migne i. p. 358.
[3] In Epist. ad Petrum de Pyrrho Constantinop.

infallibility was *all but explicitly defined;* and we could not give a more convincing proof of the belief of the early Church than is found in what took place at that Council and after it.

The one to which we refer, the fourth of Constantinople, the eighth Œcumenical Council, met in 869, just before the Photian schism. Now Pope Hadrian II. sent over a profession of faith, with orders that no one should be allowed to sit in the Council without first subscribing it, and this condition was accepted. The document contains these words : " The first condition of salvation is to hold the right rule of faith and in no way deviate from the decrees of the Fathers . . . and because the sentence of our Lord Jesus Christ, who said " thou art Peter " etc., cannot be passed over, what was there said is proved by the result of events : for in the Apostolic See religion has always been preserved immaculate and so has the pure doctrine of Catholicism." This formula—known under the name of " Formula of Pope Hormisdas," because in 519 it was drawn up by that Pope and was subscribed by the Emperor, the patriarch and the bishops of the East—was copied and signed by about a hundred Eastern bishops, not to speak of the others who sat at the last session of the Council; according to Dollinger it was thus signed in all by about 2,500 Eastern bishops.[1] Now nearly four-fifths of those who signed it at the eighth General Council were bishops who had fallen into heresy and supported Photius; who consequently would have willingly seized upon this occasion of attacking their judge, the Bishop of Rome, if there had been in his assertion anything against the common belief of those days. They signed it, and thus agreed that the Roman See had always been free from error in matters of faith. They confessed that the promise made by Christ accounted for it in the past ; they declared that the said promise could not be passed over, but was sure to be realized; therefore they implicitly declared that it would ever be realized and that, as a consequence, the Roman See would always preserve the pure doctrine; which was tantamount to saying that the Bishop of Rome, who taught in that See, was infallible.

---

[1] Hist. of the Church, vol. ii. p. 221.

But we have here not only the belief of doctors in the infallibility of the Pope, we have a declaration made in a General Council (Act. 1) by bishops who all understood it to bear on points of faith and doctrine, as its aim was to induce them to condemn heretics, because their doctrine was opposed to that of the Roman Church and had been condemned in Rome. Hence we have said that this eighth Œcumenical Council did all but explicitly define the Pope's infallibility.

All we have said shows obviously that the early Church looked upon the Roman Bishop as one who could not but teach the truth in matters of doctrine, in other words, as one who was infallible.[1]

Now *this conviction has to be accounted for*, and we are of opinion that what we said of the belief in the Pope's supremacy must be repeated here : only one thing can account for it, namely, the teaching of our Lord and His Apostles. To our mind the belief in those two prerogatives implies that they taught that Peter was to have successors as head of the Church, and that these were to have like him a privilege of infallibility ; it implies also that, if not Christ, at least the Apostles declared that the Roman Bishop was to be considered as head of the fold and as such would be endowed with a privilege of immunity from error in matters of doctrine. Nothing else, so far as we are able to see, can account for the belief of the early centuries either in the supremacy or the infallibility of the Roman Pontiff.

---

[1] Even supposing that St. Cyprian wrote the letters which are attributed to him, and looked upon the question of re-baptism as one of doctrine and not of discipline (two points which are far from being proved); supposing that he did act and speak according to his conviction, and did really disbelieve the Pope's infallibility, (though he wrote that "the Roman Bishop had always been the channel between Christ and the Church, distributing to all the Divine teaching,") the fact that so great a bishop had but a few in his own time, and practically none after him, to share his view, is a clear proof that his opinion was looked upon as incorrect and contrary to the general teaching of the early Church.

The Easter question was not doctrinal. But the fact that Rome settled it and the way it was settled show that the Papal supremacy was not denied in the second or in the seventh century, even by those who could oppose to the regulations sent by Rome the practice of several Apostles and, in the case of Ireland, that of the early Church. (Cf. Euseb. Hist. Eccl. lib. v., cc. 23 24; Spicileg. Solesm. tom. i., pp 10 and 11 ; Bedæ Hist. Eccl. Angl. lib. ii., c. 19 ; lib. iii., c. 25.)

The "Natural Causes" Theory.

Five causes have been mentioned as favourable to the influential position of the Pope in the early centuries, viz., the Clementine Romance, the fact that Rome was the first city of the empire, the substitution of the papal for the imperial court, the wealth and bounty of the Roman Church, and the intellectual ignorance and dulness which led her to assert ridiculous rights and then prevented her seeing or admitting that they were groundless. But we do not think that any of these can account for the belief in the Pope's supremacy, much less in his infallibility. (Cf. The Roman Claim to Supremacy by Dr. Moorhouse, 1894.)

(*a*) The *Clementines* tell us that Peter was the first Bishop of Rome; and on this assertion, according to those who differ from us, the Popes based their claims to the supremacy and infallibility: therefore they add, as the Clementines are not the work of St. Clement, the Popes' claims are based upon forgery and ignorance. (Cf. Salmon, Lightfoot, also Puller's Primitive Saints, etc., p. 46).

If the Clementines are truly the only proof we have that Peter was Bishop of Rome, we are willing to admit that his episcopate in that city is questionable, since those Homilies and Recognitions of St. Clement are a spurious work. However, since even apocryphal productions may at times tell the truth, it is not proved yet that Peter never was Bishop of Rome. But even if he was not, it does not follow that the Bishop of Rome was not rightly looked upon in those days as head of the Church. This conviction cannot have rested merely on the assertion of the Clementines, which assertion might indeed explain why the primitive Church believed that Peter was Bishop of Rome, but could not show why she considered his successors as head of the fold of Christ. The Bishops of Jerusalem also succeeded an Apostle, yet were never regarded as supreme shepherds of the universal Church. We could not account for this by saying that Peter only was the head of the Church, while St. James was not; for the assertion of the Clementines does not explain why any bishop was thought to have inherited such a prerogative; nor does it explain why the bishops of Antioch, who also were Peter's successors, never claimed to be and were never looked upon as being each in turn the head of the Church. All this tends to show that the Popes' claims can hardly have been based merely on the few words of the Clementines, as from them one could only conclude that Peter had been Bishop of Rome, not that his successors were the head of the Church or infallible.

But it is true to say—and this practically removes the objection—that the Roman Bishops were looked upon both as Peter's successors and as the head of the Church, by the very doctors and bishops who considered the Clementines as spurious.[1] Eusebius (+ about 315), St. Athanasius (+ 373) apud Migne, vol. xxvii. p. 431, St. Jerome (+420) in de Viris Ill. c. 1, Pope Gelasius, and the Roman Council in 495, declare the work spurious, yet hold that Peter was Bishop of Rome and that the Bishop of Rome is the head of the Church. The mere fact that the Romans claimed Peter, a Jew, an ignorant fisherman, as their bishop, instead of Paul, a Roman citizen and an eloquent orator, and that the patriarch of Constantinople accepted the Pope's supremacy, is evidence enough that the Pope's supremacy was not based on a lie.

(*b*) Can the fact that Rome was the *first city of the Empire* account for the Papal supremacy? No: for no Pope ever appeals to that fact or calls himself the bishop of the imperial city: in reality, Rome is more often called the "Apostolic See" than the "Imperial City" by Christians. It may be added that the Bishops of Constantinople never claimed jurisdiction over the whole world, still less infallibility, even when Rome had ceased to be the capital of the empire and the emperors had removed their throne to Constantinople: they only claimed the second place, and that only in the order of distinction and honour.

(*c*) That the *substitution of the Papal for the imperial court* allowed the Pope's dignity to assume greater proportions in the eyes of the Romans, no one will question; but it does not

[1] Or who could hardly have heard of the Clementines. If the Clementines first became known between A.D. 160 and 170, it is not certain that they were known to Tertullian (+200), who wrote that Clement was ordained by Peter; or to St. Irenæus (160-240) and St. Cyprian (+250), whose words we have given (pp. 74-76), and who mention (Iren. Hær. iii., 11; Cypr. Epist. 55) that Peter was Bishop of Rome At all events, it is unlikely that they were in existence when St. Clement (+101?) wrote the words we quoted above (p. 76); or when St. Ignatius of Antioch (+between 105 and 117) and Hegesippus (+160) asserted that Peter ruled the Roman Church. See S. Ign. Epist. ad Rom.; Heges. ap. Euseb. H. E. lib. iv. c. 22. Cf. Dr. Lightfoot, in the *Academy*, May 21, 1887; Fr. Livius's St. Peter Bishop of Rome, part 1. Burns and Oates, 1888.

follow that, in the eyes of other cities and nations, the Bishop of Rome became any greater, because his city was no longer the metropolis of the empire. We should rather have expected the opposite : the pastor of a great city is more likely to have influence than that of a less important one. Yet it is not the Bishop of Constantinople, but the Bishop of Rome, who is looked upon as the head of the Church.

(*d*) Some affirm that the Bishop of Rome obtained his influence because his *Church was wealthy* and in a position to render considerable assistance to other Churches in less favourable circumstances. The bounty of the Roman Church to needy Churches cannot be denied ; nevertheless we must observe that even wealthy sees, as that of Constantinople, recognised the Pope's supremacy, and we know that some of them were most jealous of their bishops' prerogatives. Unless all bishops were, for several centuries, hopelessly corrupt, we cannot believe that they unanimously agreed to barter their independence to Rome for some temporal advantages offered to needy cities, and that not one bishop rose to protest against the mistake, or the crime, of handing over supreme and absolute authority to the See of Rome. It is strange that they never proposed in a Council to appoint the powerful Bishop of Constantinople as their head ; not even in any of the Eastern Councils was such an idea suggested, though, as in the eighth Œcumenical they might have found a majority unfavourable to the Roman Pontiff.

(*e*) Have the *intellectual ignorance and dulness* of the Roman Church led her to assert and claim ridiculous rights? Such ignorance and dulness being granted, it would be strange indeed that she should even have conceived the idea of them, yet stranger if, in spite of her stupidity, she had succeeded in making all the other Churches and learned doctors recognise them ; for among those who acknowledged her privileges are to be found sees as that of Constantinople, and men of superior virtue, like St. Jerome, St. Augustine, St. Chrysostom, St. Cyril of Alexandria, etc. : ignorance and dulness seldom lead to success.

" She could never see that her claims were groundless." We admit the fact, but attribute it to a keen sense of the truth or to a divine intervention which preserved her from ever being misled by sophisms.

" Her dulness," it is said, " made it impossible for her to

own her mistake and alter her belief." Such an explanation is a double-edged sword: if any one asserts that she was too dull ever to deny what she had once believed, he implicitly grants that she believed, and consequently was taught from the very first, that the Bishop of Rome enjoyed the prerogatives she claimed; for had she at first been taught the contrary, her inborn stupidity would certainly have prevented her from ever accepting a different view.

We have shown that none of those causes are able to account for the general recognition of the Pope's supremacy and infallibility throughout the early centuries; therefore it only remains for us to attribute the origin of that belief to the teaching of our Lord and of the Apostles.

Indeed, unless we do this, we must own that the primitive Church fell into *error in matters of doctrine;* for her authorised teachers certainly led the faithful to believe that Christ meant Peter to have, till the end of time, successors who should be, like him, infallible and the head of His whole fold.

However, as the Church cannot fall into error in matters of faith (p. 52), it follows that her belief in the early centuries was *not erroneous*, and consequently that Christ did really mean Peter to have successors till the end of the world. Nay more, since the teachers as a body are infallible and taught that doctrine, we may conclude that it was all but defined from the very first centuries. A man who would have refused to accept it, would not have been actually guilty of an act of rebellion against lawful authority and cut off from the fold, because the Church had actually passed no ecclesiastical law binding him to believe it and making this a condition of membership. But he would have been denying *the truth*, a *revealed truth* proposed by the authority appointed by Christ, and so would have been guilty of a *sin against faith*, unless excused by ignorance. (Cf. Palmieri, de Rom. Pont. p. 633; Ballerini-Palmieri, tom. ii. pp. 54 seq.)

Art. III.—**The fact that a particular teacher is at least tacitly recognised by Peter or his successors, is the common and conclusive proof that he is authorised by Christ.**

After what we said above (p. 47), this requires no demonstration: it follows from the fact that Christ did make His Church a *monarchy* with Peter and his successors as a head, and that miracles can be only an exception and are not to be expected without necessity.

Consequences.

Before bringing this chapter to a close, we beg leave to draw the reader's attention to a few important consequences of the doctrine we have tried to demonstrate.

1. Since the teaching body established by Christ was meant to exist till the end of time, it certainly *exists at the present day*.

2. Since the sheep and lambs, i.e. the whole fold, were placed by Christ under one head, and since that head was intended to exist till the end of the world, it follows that *the head of the Church will never disappear*.

It follows also that the fold cannot and never will have more than *one head at a time;* for if a portion of it could possibly be under a second head, the fold would no longer be what Christ wished it to be, a society of men under one head. Consequently a so-called second pope can be but an intruder and a usurper, and cannot have any divine supremacy over the fold or over a portion of it.

From the same fact results a third consequence, namely, that the true fold is not a society made up of independent communities or of independent national churches; *the true fold is a monarchy*, i.e., a society of men who, believing Christ's doctrine and partaking of the means of sanctification or sacraments He has instituted, recognise as their superior one man, viz., Peter and his successors. Therefore, as no one can be said to belong to a society, if he will not recognise and obey the supreme authority that rules over it, likewise no one belongs to the true fold of Christ who does not recognise and obey, as his superior, Peter or his successor, whoever this may be at the time.

3. As Ferraris says (Biblioth. art. Papa, p. 949), the Church of Christ cannot *err in recognising a man as her head*, as otherwise she might happen to listen to one who, being a spurious head, has not the privilege of infallibility, and so would be hopelessly exposed to the danger of erring in doctrine; nay, she would actually do so in regarding a fallible man as the infallible rule of faith.[1]

---

[1] Cf. Schmalzgrueber, Jus. Eccl. Min. vol. i. p. 11, tit. vi. 98; also Dr. Littledale's Theory of the Disappearance of the Papacy, by Sydney Smith. London: 126, Kennington Park Road, S.E.

4. The Church of Christ being a monarchy, *no one can have authority*, i.e. a right to teach, judge or rule over any part of it, unless he is either appointed, or at least tacitly recognised for this purpose by the head of the Church; even the Apostles, who had received their appointment and authority from Christ Himself, could not exercise it, except in due subordination to Peter and his successors: for without this the head could not be said to have full authority and jurisdiction over all. As a matter of fact, in that form of civil society which is called a monarchy, no one has authority to render judgment, to interpret the law, to rule and govern, who has not been duly appointed, or who, once appointed, has been afterwards deprived of his authority by the monarch or his representatives. He may succeed in invading a province or an office, or in keeping them against the will of the Sovereign; but his intrusion or rebellion will give him no rights; vainly will the people, through ignorance or fear, address themselves to him; he will still be nothing but a *usurper*. Likewise should such usurpations or intrusions be found in the spiritual monarchy called the Church, the guilty parties would have no right to teach or rule; they might succeed in gathering round them supporters and followers, as Nestorius and Photius did in the see of Constantinople; they might, after being deprived of their authority, continue to live in the same houses, teach and rule in the same churches, make and appoint teachers as they had done before; nay more, after a time their successors might feel convinced they were duly authorised teachers, and rulers; they might even do a great work for souls by their teaching and example—God thus rewarding their own good faith and intentions, and that of their followers. Yet in the eyes of God, they would be only usurpers and rebels, refusing to submit to their lawful superior. Christ, who wishes Peter and his successors to have full authority over His whole fold, could not, without contradicting Himself, approve of any one teaching and ruling independently of them; He would not, and could not, be with men denying obedience to the authority He has Himself established; He could not give them, without being inconsistent, an authority insubordinate to that of Peter and of his successors; still less a right to condemn one single point of the doctrine taught by the Prince of the Apostles and his successors, as this would be giving them a right to deny the truth and implicitly to spread error. Peter

and his successors being infallible in their teaching, any one condemning their creed and implicitly upholding the opposite, is undoubtedly rejecting the truth and indirectly teaching error. Such intruders and usurpers, and their supporters and followers, are evidently going against Christ's wishes, nay, doing what He can only disapprove of and forbid.

5. If any one wish to *know Christ's doctrine* without fear ot being misled, reason will tell him to apply to that body of men authorised by our Saviour to propagate it, and endowed with infallibility to effect this purpose ; it will tell him that he is not to apply to those who teach independently of the head of the Church or without at least his tacit approval, as such men remain unauthorised and therefore offer no real guarantee that they know and impart the truth.

6. If above all a man wish *to do the will of Christ*, he will apply for information about His doctrine to the teaching body appointed by Him for the very purpose of making it known. His having appointed them for that object clearly implies that He wishes all men to listen to them : "He that heareth you heareth Me; he that despiseth you despiseth Me."

7. Since our Lord has given one man full authority to teach and govern both the pastors and the flock, i.e., the whole Church, *every one is bound* to accept that man's doctrine and follow his directions; and as our Saviour made his authority depend on no condition, no one can ever be justified in starting an *independent* branch or denomination and in refusing to obey the head of the Church or accept his teaching as the pure Gospel of Christ.

CHAPTER VI.

WHERE THAT MEANS IS TO BE FOUND AT THE PRESENT DAY.

WE have proved from historical documents that Christ has appointed an infallible teaching authority under one infallible head as the means to impart His doctrine and religion to the world; and—for such as may hold that history is no safe guide to settle any question, since it can be made to prove opinions diametrically opposed—we have shown that any man consulting his common sense is sure to arrive at the same conclusion.

We have also clearly demonstrated that, since Christ wishes all men to know His teaching, the means appointed by Him for that purpose will exist till the end of time, and therefore exists at the present day. But now comes this practical question: Where is that means to be found?

To our mind, if the means appointed by Christ are such as we described, there cannot be any doubt that the following must be the answer: (1) The teaching authority constituted by our Lord is not found outside the Catholic Church,[1] because every teaching body or denomination, outside the Catholic Church, disclaims the possession of an infallible head. (2) It is found in the Catholic Church, because the teaching body in that Church, and the Church herself, claim to be ruled and taught by one infallible man.

I.—It is not found outside the Catholic Church.

1. Ask any Christian, whether a layman or a clergyman, outside the Catholic Church, if there is in his denomination a *supreme head*, or if that head is considered to be *infallible* in his teaching: to one of these questions, if not to both of them, you are sure to get a negative answer; and this answer will

---

[1] By which we mean what some call the "Roman Catholic persuasion."

prove of itself that the means is not to be found in any denomination outside the Catholic Church.

If, for the sake of curiosity, you inquire further whether those who teach in his Church are infallible as *a body*, you will most probably again receive a negative answer. An English Churchman, quoting Article XXI., will perhaps add that "even Councils may err in the things pertaining unto God: wherefore things ordained by them have neither strength nor authority, unless it may be declared" (by whom? and when is this declaration free from error?) "that they be taken from Holy Scriptures." Some may say that a General Council of all the Christian bishops in the world would be infallible; but of course this would not prove that the infallible teaching body is found outside the Catholic Church; for in the case of such a Council, the bishops would by a large majority be Catholic bishops, with the Pope as their head.

2. One could not object that some Christian denominations might possess an infallible teaching authority under one infallible head, without being aware of it; since, unfortunately for this opinion, every one of the Christian denominations outside the Catholic Church denies its own infallibility and that of the man, when such a man exists, who may happen to be considered as its head; even this very head denies at the present day his own infallibility in matters of doctrine, so that if a particular denomination or its head should at some future period claim to be infallible, we have at the present day error on a point of doctrine, taught by *that very denomination* and by its head, since they teach that no individual, no society, is infallible! This alone would show that *they* do not possess that prerogative

II.—It is found in the Catholic Church.

The Catholic Church *claims* to be infallible and to have an infallible head; she is the only one to make such a claim, the only one that does not deny her own infallibility and that of her head, indeed the only one whose head claims to be infallible: this fact alone points out that she must possess the infallible teachers appointed by Christ to impart His doctrine. For if the teaching authority appointed by Christ *must be found somewhere*, and is not found outside the Catholic Church, it follows that it must be found in her, since Christ meant it to exist till the end of time.

We have seen what the prerogatives of the teachers must be, if the end Christ has in view is to be obtained; we have seen also what the prerogatives were which Christ actually granted to those men: the Catholic Church claims these prerogatives for her teachers. "One must believe," says the Vatican Council (A.D. 1870), "with a divine and catholic faith, what the Church, either by a solemn judgment, or by her ordinary and universal teaching, proposes to our belief as divinely revealed" (sess. iii. ch. 3). This clearly implies the claim that *her Pastors*, not as individuals but *as a body, are* in such a case *infallible*.

She claims to possess *a head* endowed with *plenary jurisdiction* over the teachers and those whom they teach: "If any shall say that the Roman Pontiff . . . . has not full and supreme power over the Universal Church, not only in things that belong to faith and morals, but also in those that relate to the discipline and government of the Church spread throughout the world; or assert that he possesses merely the principal part and not all the fulness of this supreme power; or that this power, which he enjoys, is not ordinary and immediate both over each and all the Churches and over each and all the pastors and the faithful: let him be anathema" (Const. Dogm. Vat. cap. iii. Card. Manning's translation). "We define," says the Council of Florence in 1439, "that the Roman Pontiff is the successor of Blessed Peter, prince of the Apostles, and the true vicar of Christ, and the head of the whole Church, and the father and doctor of all Christians; and to him in Blessed Peter was delivered by our Lord Jesus Christ the plenary power of feeding, ruling and governing the Universal Church, as it is contained in the acts of the Œcumenical Councils and the sacred Canons."

She claims that the Roman Pontiff is infallible in the following decree of the Vatican Council, sanctioned by Pope Pius IX. "We, the sacred Council approving, teach and define that it is a dogma divinely revealed, that the *Roman Pontiff* when he speaks *ex cathedra*,—that is, when, discharging the office of pastor and teacher of all Christians, by reason of his supreme apostolic authority, he defines a doctrine regarding faith and morals to be held by the whole Church—he, by the divine assistance promised to him in Blessed Peter, possesses that *infallibity* with which the Divine Redeemer willed that His Church should be endowed in defining a doctrine regarding faith or morals, and that therefore such definitions of the said Roman Pontiff are of themselves unalterable and not from the consent of the Church " (Vatic. Council, sess. iv. ch. 4, July 18, 1870).

The Church does not assert that the Roman Pontiff is impeccable: indeed, her doctors discuss what should be done, if he were an unjust cruel tyrant; she does not claim that, though he can validly deprive a bishop of all jurisdiction, he is at liberty to do so without reason: for right order does not allow a superior to do all that can be validly done by him; and in this present case in particular it only requires that every teacher and ruler should have at least his tacit approval. Nor does she say that he is infallible in every statement he may choose to make, but only in matters of faith and morals, and provided he intends to define what doctrine the whole Church must hold; for if he does not mean to teach and bind the Universal Church, he may fall into error and even heresy like any one else. As to matters that have nothing to do with revealed truth or man's sanctification, she claims no infallibility either for her head or for her teachers as a body, though she holds that the Pope can infallibly decide whether or not a certain truth comes within the scope of his infallible teaching. But it is a function of the Apostolate not only to teach and declare revealed truth against direct denial, but also to safeguard it against indirect attacks, no matter from what quarter they may come; besides, natural truth is often closely interlaced with the supernatural, indeed so closely connected that both stand or fall together, so that those who hold the Apostolic office, the Pope and the bishops in union with him, may often have to pass doctrinal and final decisions even upon natural truths: hence, though it is not defined by the Church whether Divine assistance (the cause of infallibility) preserves such doctrinal decisions from error, or whether the human ecclesiastical authority of the Church is a sufficient guarantee of their truth or falsehood, theologians generally hold that her teachers as a body, and the Pope by himself are infallible in those decisions; they hold, for instance, that they are infallible when declaring the names and number of the Books that contain the revealed doctrine; when defining natural truths that are postulated for the proper teaching of supernatural doctrine (for example, this natural truth, " Revelation is possible "); when drawing conclusions partly from revealed truths and partly from truths that are not revealed (such as the following conclusion, " Man is ruled by the moral law," since he is free—a revealed truth—and since every free being is ruled by the moral law—a natural truth proclaimed by reason) ; again, when ascribing a doctrine to a certain book or writer ; or directing all the faithful to honour a departed saint, as one already with God in heaven ; or approving of a rule of life, as being in accordance with the teaching of Christ ; or making regulations for the whole Church about a certain exterior work referring to the worship of God or to the spiritual good of souls (for instance, such regulations as have to do with the administration of sacraments, the celibacy of the clergy—Acts xv. 25 and 28) ; or, again, tolerating a general practice closely and directly connected with belief (for example, prayer for the dead, which is directly connected with the belief in Purgatory).

We think we have made it clear that the Catholic Church of the present day claims to possess those very prerogatives and privileges which our reason assures us Christ must have given, and which history says He gave to the teachers He appointed to spread His doctrine till the end of time. We also believe that what we have stated will enable the reader to solve any difficulties and objections which may present themselves to his mind, and which, as we are anxious to be brief, we forbear to mention. Of one, however, we will take notice. Modern Popes, it is said, have far more authority than the early Popes ; therefore, they *modified the constitution* given by Christ to His Church. Our answer is that in the early centuries the Popes thought fit not to use all their authority, or indeed found it actually impossible to exercise it fully. At the present day it has become easier for them to discharge in person the duties of their office, and accordingly they prefer doing so. They may seem sometimes to encroach upon the rights of bishops ; but in reality they do not, for unlike the rights of the Apostles which came directly from Christ, those of bishops are bestowed upon them by the head of the Church, since Christ made His Church a monarchy and gave Peter and his successors full and complete jurisdiction over the whole flock ; like the Apostles, modern bishops are subordinate to the head of the Church, but besides receive their jurisdiction from him. Bishops there must be; but it does not follow that they must have the same power as the Apostles: even in the times of the latter, they had not the universal jurisdiction enjoyed by each member of the Apostolic College. The head of the Church may limit their power, or make it depend upon the fulfilment of certain conditions unheard of in the early centuries, such as his direct sanction to their election; but whether he limits or extends that jurisdiction, whether he gives more or less independence to the various heads of national Churches, he is using his right as a supreme monarch and not encroaching upon the rights of others. (Cf. D. Grea, L'Église et sa Divine Constitution, pp. 242 seq.)

Conclusion.

I.—If the reader be convinced that Christ offers us in the teaching of the Catholic Church the means of knowing what He wishes us to believe and to do in order to be saved, the following conclusions will force themselves upon him:—

1. *Every one* has in the teaching of that Church the *means of knowing* Christ's doctrine and religion.

2. Any one *wishing to know* what our Lord has taught must apply to the priests and bishops approved by the Pope —or to the Roman Pontiff himself—since they are the teachers authorised by Christ and as a body are endowed with infallibility, while as individuals, by the fact that they are authorised by the Bishop of Rome or in his name, they offer us a real guarantee that they know and will teach the truth. Nay more, under certain circumstances, the Pope himself is infallible.

3. Any one *anxious to do God's will* must apply for information about Christ's religion to the Roman Pontiff or to teachers authorised by him, since our Lord undoubtedly wishes us to make use of the means He has appointed for the spreading of His doctrine.

4. Every one is *bound* to apply for information about the teaching of Christ to the Pope or to the doctors authorised by him; because it is his duty to avoid the risk of denying what our Saviour taught, and wishes or even binds us to believe—

and that is the only safe way to avoid such a danger, no other teachers being infallible either as a body or as individuals.

5. To listen to and follow teachers not authorised by the Bishop of Rome is, to say the least, *imprudent*, as such men can hardly offer any serious guarantee that they know and will teach the pure doctrine of Christ.

6. To refuse to hear the Pope and those whom he authorises as teachers, is not only imprudent—it is going *against the will of God;* for since our Lord has appointed them to teach His doctrine, He naturally wishes that all should listen to them. Indeed, of those who would disdain them as teachers, He said : "He that despiseth you, despiseth Me."

II.—**We have also established in the course of our study that the Roman Pontiff holds from Christ full and plenary jurisdiction over the entire Church.** If the reader look upon this as sufficiently proved, then again he must admit the following consequences :—

1. *No one may* teach Christ's doctrine or exercise spiritual jurisdiction without at least the tacit or implicit consent of the Bishop of Rome. Consequently, if a man has never received that consent, or if it is implicitly or explicitly denied him, he has no right either to rule or teach. He may, therefore, be a true bishop, and may have been duly authorised to govern a diocese and teach Christ's doctrine, but he has ceased to be a real successor of the Apostles. On the one hand, he is no longer what every Apostle is, one of the authorised teachers and rulers, since he is deprived of his authority by him who alone had power to give it ; on the other hand, Christ has not granted him a special mission to spread His doctrine and govern the faithful, since He wishes all men to hear His Apostles and their legitimate successors and could not at the same time wish the opposite, viz., that they should listen to one who is neither an Apostle nor one of their successors. Indeed He could not give that man a special mission in opposition to, or even merely independent of, the Pope, since he has constituted the latter the head of His Church and binds every one to submit to his authority.

2. To exercise jurisdiction, or teach the doctrine of Christ independently or in spite of the Bishop of Rome, is an act of *intrusion or rebellion* against lawful authority.

3. *To listen to or support* one who has not at least the tacit approval of the Roman Pontiff, in other words, to belong to any other religious body than the Catholic Church, is fundamentally wrong and against the will of God, as it is to support teachers or rulers that knowingly or through ignorance deny obedience to lawful authority.

4. Any one anxious to become a *member of the religious society* founded by Christ, must submit to the Pope's authority as exercised by himself or by the bishops and priests he approves.

5. Any one desirous to *do Christ's will* must follow the same course.

6. To deny obedience to the Roman Pontiff and to the bishops authorised by him and thus remain outside the Catholic Church is to go against Christ's will; it is also an act of rebellion, since the Pope is the lawful superior appointed by our Lord over all men; and such a course must be *fundamentally wrong.*

How far a man may be guilty, we can judge from the words of our Saviour: "If he will not hear the Church, let him be to thee as the heathen and publican" (Matt. xviii. 17); "He that despiseth you, despiseth Me" (Luke x. 15); or from what the Apostles said on the subject, and of this we can form an idea either by reading what the early Christians were taught, or, still better, by listening to what the Pope, the infallible guide, taught on the subject.

"He who joins himself to a sectary shall have no inheritance in the kingdom of God," writes St. Ignatius, martyr, who died between A.D. 105 and 117. "Any one outside the Church, will escape, if any outside Noah's Ark could escape," says St. Cyprian. [1] " A man that is a heretic avoid, knowing that he that is such a one is subverted. He who has severed himself from the Church must be avoided and shunned. Such a one is subverted and sinneth, being condemned by his own judgment." [2] " Being outside the Church," says St. Augustine, "separated from the frame of unity and the bonds of love, you will be punished with everlasting tortures, even if you willingly

---

[1] c. 6, 17. [2] Tit. iii. 11, as quoted by St. Cyprian, de Unit. cc. 6 and 17.

give yourselves up to be burned alive for the name of Christ."[1] "Hold this unhesitatingly," says Fulgentius of Ruspe (A.D. 467—533), "that not merely the heathen, but Jews also and heretics and schismatics who live out of the Catholic Church, shall go into everlasting fire."[2] In more recent times, Pope Boniface VIII. says: "We declare it to be necessary to salvation that every human creature should be subject to the Roman Pontiff."[3] "There is but one universal Church of the faithful, and outside it no one at all is saved," says the Fourth Council of the Lateran, c. 1. "We must hold it to be of faith," writes Pope Pius IX., "that no one outside the Apostolic Roman Church can be saved ; for she is the one ark of salvation. He who enters her not, will perish in the flood."[4] The same Pope had said in his first Encyclical: "Out of the Church there is no salvation.[5]

7. Therefore we must judge of those who refuse to be exteriorly members of the Catholic Church as of men who do something wrong in itself ; they are responsible, guilty and *liable to punishment according to the degree of their knowledge and freedom.*—Consequently any one who is aware of his obligation to join the Catholic Church and is free to do so, but refuses to comply with that obligation, is guilty of grave sin ; which means that for him there is no salvation possible, unless he become a member of the Catholic Church.—What excuses him from the obligation of joining it, excuses him also from the sin and its consequences. Therefore a man may and will be saved outside the Catholic Church, no matter to what Christian denomination he may belong, nay more, even if he be no Christian at all, provided that the two following conditions are fulfilled in him, viz., first, that he be ignorant of

---

[1] St. Aug. Epist. 173, 6 ; de Baptismo, 3, 16 ; 4, 24 ; Sermo ad Cæsar. Eccles. no. 6.
[2] De fide ad Petrum c. 39 ; Hageman, Römisch. Kirche, p. 9.
[3] Extrav. comm. l. I., tit. 8, c. 1.
[4] Quoted by Schanz, Christian Apology, iii. p. 288, English transl.
[5] Even Luther and Calvin declare that outside the true Church—which according to them is not the Catholic Church—there is no salvation: "That all in communion with him [the Pope] are lost is an article of faith, wherever genuine Calvinism is rampant. It stands in the Westminster Confession," writes Döllinger (Kirche, pp. 277, 286). How long may one put off joining the Catholic Church without committing a grievous sin? See answer in Lehmkuhl, tom. ii. No. 77, edit. 5ᵃ ; cf. St. Thomas In 4. disp. 17, q. 3, art. 1, § 4 ; Ballerini-Palmieri, v. p. 557 ; Billuart, viii. diss. iii., art. vi.

the obligation binding upon all to enter the Catholic Church, or that he be unable to do so; second, that besides, he be in a state of grace, which our Lord compares to the "wedding garment," in other words, provided he satisfy to the best of his present abilities the strict obligation of belonging to the true fold. But let it be remembered that nothing but perfect charity or contrition can give the "wedding garment," the life of grace, to a man who is not validly baptised or who after baptism has fallen into some grievous fault. And perfect charity or real contrition cannot exist in one who refuses to fulfil any of the important precepts given by God to man, amongst which, as we have just said, is the obligation to belong to the Catholic Church.— A man who does what he thinks he ought to do and avoids what he believes he should avoid, will certainly receive from God a special grace, so that he may die clothed with the wedding garment. "Were a man," says St. Thomas, "bred in the woods or amongst the beasts, to follow the natural instinct of his reason by desiring good and avoiding evil, God would certainly make known to such a one what he must believe, either by an immediate revelation or by sending a special messenger, as He sent Peter to Cornelius" (de Verit. q. xiv a. 11, ad 1).

But what *if a man has doubts* whether the Catholic Church be the true Church of Christ or not? Is such a one bound under pain of damnation to make enquiries, or can he be saved if he neglect to remove his doubts and meanwhile remain outside the true fold?

As such a man wilfully exposes himself to the danger of violating the obligation of belonging to the Church, which, as we have seen, is a most serious one, it is evident that his negligence or wilful imprudence is radically wrong, and that in certain cases it may be so deliberate and grave as to amount to a grievous fault; which means that he may be guilty of mortal sin and so lose his soul, if he do not make sufficient efforts to clear up his doubts.—However, should he fail in his efforts to remove them, reason will bind him, when on his deathbed, to follow what to him appears to be the safer course, as there is no more time to inquire, and when it is a question of salvation, we are commanded by common sense to adopt the safer policy. [1]

[1] Cf. Sanchez, decal. lib. 2. cap. i. no. 5, 6; Ballerini-Palmieri, tom. ii. pp. 17-18.

But even though no such interest as salvation were at stake, the fact that Christ will be pleased and honoured by a man's endeavouring to find out which Church is the fold that all must join, should induce every earnest Christian that may happen to have doubts, to try to clear them up.

Vainly would he refuse to make enquiries on the plea that others more learned than he feel safe to remain where they are; for others again equally learned and conscientious felt that they were bound to join the Catholic Church in order not to forfeit their salvation; these had everything to gain in not breaking their connexion with their own denomination, and were consequently sure to discuss every argument most attentively before giving up those advantages; so that if he were blindly to follow any one's example, his reason would almost oblige him to imitate the latter, as having more likely studied the question with greater care. Should he object to this course, he must, in order not to be condemned by his own reason and by God, make enquiries for himself, i.e. study and consult,—and above all humbly ask the Almighty to enlighten him and give him grace to follow his conscience, whatever it may move him to do. Prayer is the most powerful means to obtain what we desire, for Christ said, "Ask and you shall receive," and there is no doubt that He will will keep His promise.

We hope we have made it clear that *there is a means of avoiding all religious divisions*, a means that reason points out to us, and that Christ has appointed and binds us to make use of. We have proved also that our Lord did not only provide us with the means of avoiding divisions in the faith by giving us an infallible teacher and binding us to accept his doctrine; His desire that we should all be one is so great that He actually wishes and obliges us to form one visible religious *society under the headship of the Bishop of Rome*. God grant that this little book may be the means of inducing many souls to comply with Christ's desire and obey His commands, so that we may be no longer "tossed to and fro and carried about with every wind of doctrine" (Eph. iv. 14), and that there may be but "one fold and one shepherd." (John x. 16).

THE END.

www.ingramcontent.com/pod-product-compliance
Lightning Source LLC
Chambersburg PA
CBHW022142160426
43197CB00009B/1403